INSIDE
THE
DYSLEXIC
MIND

Other books by Laughton King

*Reaching the Reluctant Learner: A manual of strategies
for teachers and parents* (third edition 2006)
With, Not Against: A compendium of parenting strategies
(second edition 2008)
*Dyslexia Dismantled: A practical breakdown for the parent,
the teacher and the dyslexic child* (2010)
www.dyslexiadismantled.com

INSIDE
THE
DYSLEXIC
MIND

A resource for
parents, teachers
and dyslexics
themselves

LAUGHTON KING

EXISLE
PUBLISHING

First published 2023

Exisle Publishing Pty Ltd
226 High Street, Dunedin, 9016, New Zealand
PO Box 864, Chatswood, NSW 2057, Australia
www.exislepublishing.com

A CiP record for this book is available from the National Library of
Australia.

ISBN: 978-1-922539-42-7

Edited by Shelley McMeeken
Designed by Shaun Jury
Typeset in Foro Sans
Printed in China

This book uses paper sourced under ISO 14001 guidelines from
well-managed forests and other controlled sources.

10 9 8 7 6 5 4 3 2 1

All names used in case studies have been altered to ensure
confidentiality.

Disclaimer
While this book is intended as a general information resource and
all care has been taken in compiling the contents, neither the author
nor the publisher and their distributors can be held responsible
for any loss, claim or action that may arise from reliance on the
information contained in this book. As each person and situation
is unique, it is the responsibility of the reader to consult a qualified
professional regarding their personal circumstances.

Contents

Important note

On each page of text, a 'ring of containment' has been strategically placed to facilitate easier participation of dyslexic readers in deciphering the meaning of the text in the book. Operating in a manner similar to that of a fence surrounding a paddock, in the writer's childhood experience, this boundary, or box, serves to help keep the letters, the words, and the reader's eyes from straying off the page during the reading process. Every little bit helps.

Preface

This book follows and complements my earlier books looking at the educational and parenting needs of children who may, or may not, have been given the label 'dyslexic'. In a similar style to my earlier books, I draw on articles I have prepared for magazines, newspapers, radio talks and public talks over my 45 years of work as a child and family psychologist.

Readers are encouraged to use the ideas, share them, develop them and send the developments back to me so that I can collate and promulgate them further. The children, their parents and their teachers need all the help they can get.

I dedicate this book and give grateful thanks to all the parents, teachers and dyslexic children who have embraced this approach to dyslexia, and whose feedback and support have made it all worthwhile.

Laughton King, 2023

Chapter One
Introduction

In Chapter One, I present some of my background and aims, and take a look at dyslexia from several angles, in order to get a general picture of the subject.

- The inside story: a portrait of a dyslexic
- Demystifying and legitimizing
- A life 'out of step'…
- Understanding our 'target group'
- Towards understanding the bigger picture
- Learning or knowledge?
- The social environment — and being politically incorrect

The inside story: a portrait of a dyslexic

Concentrating on the muscles of one eye, the one nearest the window, he knew that sometimes, if he stretched his bottom jaw down, and a bit to the other side, he could manage to hold that eye open, and sort of blink with the other eye and, yes, he could wink with both eyes — really, with one eye, and then with the other one, at different times.

The one on the classroom side of his face was easy, and he often winked with that one just to prove he could, and to practise which one was which. When he said to himself, 'Wink right,' he could tell which one was his right eye, because that was the easy one. 'Wink left' didn't come out of his mouth very well, as it wasn't so easy to say or do. He gave up even trying to say 'Wink left' out loud, but that was okay because now he knew that he could wink with both eyes — at different times — if he had to.

And this was the way that he taught himself 'right' and 'left'.

Again, he started to concentrate on the muscles he had to pull, hold or stretch, focusing so that he could get that eye to ... completely unaware that the teacher, and the whole of Room 4, were watching, waiting, once more enjoying cheap entertainment at his expense.

It was always the total silence that brought him back to their world. He could block the noise of the classroom out of his head, and the teacher's voice. The strings of words that poured endlessly from her mouth would numb his brain, but when it changed to silence, it boomed cavernously through his ears, wrenching him starkly back to their world.

His head was still held twisted high as he sought the muscles to sequence, face suddenly flushed, pumped hot, then cold, his eyes connecting with those of 34 other ten-year-olds staring at him. He froze, suddenly wanting to pee.

For Ernest this was his regular crucifixion. No day went past when his body, his mind, his actions did not let him down in some similar way. Distracted with a fascination of what its bits can do, responding to sudden surges of muscle activity, drifting off into internal picture-shows, his body kept him marked as the class nut-case — earning him more and more intense taunts, teasing, jeering from his classmates and cutting sarcasm from the teacher, fuelling them on. She was so good at that.

'Stut' they would call him, 'stut the nut' or 'stutter nutter'. Their heads held high, twisted, wild-eyed in mockery, the playground torture ensured his school-day nightmare was total.

At least for Ernest 'Stut' was better than that stupid poncy name that his parents had given him. Yes, he knew why the kids called him that, but at least it was his name, and not that stupid name that he shared with his father, and his grandfather. No kid wants to be called by the same name as his old man!

'Don't you ever let me hear you calling me your "old man" — that is a term of no respect.' Yeah, okay, I won't let you hear. I'll just say it inside my mouth, or out loud when I'm riding my bike, and you won't hear.

Sticks and stones may break my bones, but the names and the teasing go on forever. After school, in the weekends, finding solace alone in the bush gullies of his native New Zealand with the moist air from the bush streams, he would seek the deep harmony that collected with the energy of those places. The power of the huge mamaku tree fern, the pūriri, and the tānekaha helped assuage the … the … the sense of torn flesh he felt at the end of each school day. This temporary healing helped, but it did little to drown out the echoes of the taunting that even his own head kept alive in the absence of his daily peer-group tormentors.

Even in his dreams Ernest knew he wasn't safe, and he feared the night-times more than the school day. At least at school he could pretend, to some degree, that it was okay, that it didn't matter, that he was part of the 'fun'. But at night, in the darkness of his sleep, there was no active input, no ability to participate, to control, to minimize. At night he was at the total mercy of his own brain, which would take over and unleash its torture on him, punishing him for being so dumb, so stupid, so inadequate and so different.

Some of the nightmares made erratic sense and were not so bad because they could be shared with his mum the next day.

Bits could be retold, described in some approximate way so as to get some emotional support and perhaps some comforting words. Most were more erratic, made up of horrific torture scenes of spikes and blades, glass and saw edges — so much like the paintings of Hieronymus Bosch that he had discovered in his early teens.

The worst were the nightmares that had no form, that were repetitive, beyond the scope of words that could not be drawn or described in any way at all. These occurred every few days, repeating the same pattern, a process, a sequence of intense emotional experiences that left him sick in the stomach and head. Initially they would come in his sleep and wake him sweating and heaving in the bed. Later, when he learned not to sleep, to avoid the nightmares, they pursued him into his waking life, first at night-time while he lay in bed, and later into his daily life, particularly at school, where once begun, no effort or distraction would stop the brutal sequence of scenes and senses as they ground through his brain.

As a child he was emotionally crippled for the twenty minutes the process would take. As an adult he learned to work on, to continue to operate, while they took their inevitable grinding course. And although in 50 years they have decreased, they have not gone away. Where do they come from, what do they represent? The closest he has ever guessed is that in some way they represent the birth process, perhaps his memory of ejection, the ultimate rejection, of the passage down the birth canal, down and out to a torture called 'life'.

At night, alone on his wire-wove bed and sodden kapok mattress (he later learned that such a mattress could hold up to 28 litres of sweat — the fluid of fear) he devised ways to fight off sleep, barely dozing, but keeping his mind racing, alert to avoid the flush of darkness that heralded the beginning of sleep and the inevitable nightmares. Some repetitive, indescribable, horrific experiences. Others where the tormenting by fellow pupils and teachers spiralled out of control, evolving, nonsensical, crashing in panic through the walls of sleep, to wake to warm pee and cold sweat in the torture-bed of his lonely, dark, bedroom cell.

Real sleep came only with the dawn, and apart from his weekend sleep-in, Ernest survived his school days averaging little more than 90 minutes sleep per night. Forty years later the intensity of the nightmares decreased, and he found that in their monthly occurrence he was at times able to take some active role in his response to their content. Now as an adult he endures them, knowing that like all pain, they too will pass.

By chance Ernest and his family lived on the outskirts of town. A sizeable stream on the boundary offered a creative play area, the water becoming a therapy for the rest of his life. Dams, eeling, boats to be fashioned from old roofing iron, sailed and sunk. Behind the local school a natural pond hosted frogs, hawthorn bushes home to thrushes, birds' nests, eggs and distrusting starlings. Beyond the paddocks steep hills rose as a cliff, drained by narrow gullies connecting to rugged bush. These beckoned with enticing aloneness and became the focus of Ernest's mental retreat. His weekends alone in the hills promised respite, and from there they reached into his school-day classroom to comfort him — and by distracting him, put him in trouble once again.

He wasn't dumb, he knew he wasn't dumb, but he couldn't think like other people did. He knew things, and he became aware that he knew things that the other kids did not know, but neither they nor the teachers seemed able to understand his words, what he was saying or what he was thinking. There didn't seem to be any words to describe what his brain knew, and in the end he learned to shut his mouth, to say nothing, and not to even try to answer the easy questions. They got him into trouble just as much as the hard ones.

One afternoon the teacher took the class to the sink unit in the corner of the classroom. After filling the sink with water, she pulled the plug and directed the children to observe the way the water spiralled around as it went down through the plughole.

'In the southern hemisphere it goes in a clockwise direction, and in the northern hemisphere, it goes the opposite way. Any comments or questions?' Ernest exuberantly offered, 'Miss, the All Blacks won their game on Saturday, and the Lions lost.'

The headmaster's strap left his hand stinging for hours, reminding him of his own stupidity for sharing his thoughts. Again and again, in his stupidity he forgot to shut his mouth, he forgot that the thoughts in his head only got him into trouble with the people he was trying to please. Even his own father, himself a school teacher in another school, told him he was a 'fat-head and smart alec' for disrupting the teacher's lesson. Nobody asked him about his comment; they just made their judgement. Had they asked, they might have learned a little about his mind, his perception and about his thinking style — but they didn't, and so both he and they remained with the belief that he was simply a stupid disruptive kid who needed to be punished.

Ernest watched the water as it spiralled down, around, in ever-decreasing circles. In his mind's eye he saw how the pattern of the water mimicked the pattern of the crowd leaving the rugby stadium in the weekend. Last Saturday, as he watched from his position in the tall tree next door, Ernest let his mind's eye rise high above the crowd. From here, like a bird, he could see the circular tracking of the large crowd, swirling in slow motion to the gates of the stadium. In the classroom sink the pattern was the same, reminding him of the rugby stadium, and then of the results of the test match in England. The teacher asked for comment, his mouth opened — and it was too late.

On Monday morning once again he was accosted by that hated exercise — 'creative writing'. Clean piece of paper, pencil in hand, date in top corner, heading done, sentence begins, 'In the weekend, I ...' Then, blank. What comes next? Pictures, sequences jumble through his mind, but no words. 'Just write down what you did in the weekend — can that be so difficult?' No words come. After twenty minutes she comes by, stands above him; he can feel the ice. 'That's not very impressive for twenty minutes' work, Ernest — you'd better hurry if you don't want to be doing it at lunchtime.'

At least if he is inside at lunchtime, he doesn't have to endure the teasing that happens out there. But to stay inside with her all day? That is torture. Either way it is torture, and he is only ten years old. He knows he has to stay at school until he is fifteen, and five more years of this is 'forever'.

'I'm thinking, I'm still thinking about it.'

'Yes, that is what you always say,' and she walked away on her rounds — both knowing that she would soon be back.

But what he said was true: he was thinking. His head was full of memories of the weekend, vivid pictures of Dad and Granddad, with the old plywood dinghy on the trailer, the Seagull outboard screwed tight on the backboard, Dad backing the trailer down the slippery concrete ramp, totally ignoring Granddad, who walking backwards, guiding, was ignorant of the sudden drop behind him into deep water. Dad didn't even see him go.

Ernest could see all of this at a glance, just as he could also see how it would have been if Granddad had been watching behind him, but he had no sense of how to turn all this information into words — especially words on paper.

'But you still haven't written anything about your weekend.' The pictures stop. The teacher and the class displace his internal picture show and his face flushes again. He pinches his willy to stop the pee wetting his pants and hopes the bell rings early.

How do you say to a sarcastic and impatient teacher that you don't know what 'think' really means, that you can't write words when you don't have any in your head? That you could draw a picture showing some of what is in your head, or even lots of pictures — but not any words.

Sometimes Ernest could see a movie picture in his head, and sometimes there were just scenes. Sometimes there were lots of movies in his head, all at the same time, and sometimes he could be part of what he was seeing, changing it, going with it, or just watching it.

What Ernest didn't recognize was that 'normal' people had some pictures, but mainly words inside their heads, and they are able to take those words and describe their thinking by writing or saying the words. In *his* head there were pictures, lots of pictures, and only pictures — and no words, making the writing task impossible. What he also didn't know was that the more upset he became, the more emotional he became, the harder it became for him to find any words at all. When the teacher demanded he speak to explain himself and his lack of writing, the words would not flow, and his mouth, his stupid, stupid mouth, would start to laugh.

One of the clearest lessons Ernest ever learned was that he was generally wrong or that he had 'got it wrong'. Somehow, he wasn't good enough.

Struggling to clear his head of all the distracting pictures, and struggling to make some effective sense of what the teacher was saying, he would invariably find that he heard about half of what she had to offer. He listened to her words for a moment or two, would process these and extract the meaning (as best he could), then tune back in, only to find that the rest of the class had gone off to lunch in the meantime. If he had been able to control her speaking rate, he may have been able to keep up with the play, but she was always in a hurry and always pushing the class along as fast as she could; the curriculum and the length of the school term simply did not allow for the likes of Ernest.

At the end of every instructional lesson would come the same old questions: 'Do you understand?' and 'Are there any questions?' Of all the kids in the class, Ernest was the fastest to learn that the first question was never allowed to be answered with a 'No'. That just got him into real trouble, generating a stream of public sarcasm that hurt so much more than the headmaster's strap. As slow a learner as he might be, he only ever made that mistake once.

The second of these teacher questions didn't ever seem to have a useful response and would always leave him feeling confused. It wasn't that he did know everything, and it wasn't even as though he didn't have any questions — the convolutions of his mind meant that he was always questioning — but not in words, and not in a way that he could make sense of to another person. For him it was more the case that if you didn't understand something, how could you have a question about it, and more than that, how could you know you didn't understand something if you didn't already have an understanding of it? So Ernest just kept quiet when these questions were asked, knowing that he didn't know what to do, but not daring to ask for help from the teacher.

'... now everyone take a clean page in your book and start writing. You have half an hour 'til lunchtime.' There was never any apparent reason that he seemed to click into the last words of the teacher. But it seemed that he always came back into tune with the classroom to hear the last bit of the instruction, and to realize that he didn't know what to do. Holding back panic, his mind would race, his ears listening to multiple conversations around the room, eyes scanning for useful cues from other children, following, copying their actions, hoping he might catch enough to pretend for long enough until he could work out what it was he was meant to be doing. Take pencil from pencil jar, clean page in *which* book, date in top corner, and 'What are you calling it, Mark?' If Mark on one side and Susan on the other both had the same heading, it was easy. If not, hard thinking and more tries to work it out.

He had long ago stopped asking for help from the teacher. That only opened the way for more torture, loud sarcasm that the other kids loved. 'So Ernest, so keen to get help, but never really trying, huh — asleep again. Is that why you come to school — to catch up on your sleep'?

Pretending that he was a bird, Ernest could sort of leave his body on the ground and go right up into the air and look down on his school, his house and on his town. From up there he could even see that his house was surrounded by other houses, and was connected to the street, like a balloon on a string, by a long driveway that crossed a little stream and ended up just opposite the big green patch that was the playground of his school.

That was the school he went to every day — because he had to — and he would leave home as late as possible, so he didn't have to pretend he was playing with somebody in the playground. Some days, rather than sit by himself, he would call out a boy's name, then run around the corner of a building, pretending he was in a game, chasing. He knew it was only pretend, but it made him feel like he was playing — a bit.

It was lucky that he could see like a bird because it meant that he never ever got lost in town, and sometimes it was useful at school too, but he wasn't quite sure how or why.

That was the way he understood the world — by looking at it and getting a picture of it in his mind. He found that he could even tell who was speaking without looking at them, because every voice made a different picture. And that was how he learned to tell which days you go to school each week, and which ones you don't.

For a long time, he hated to go to bed each night, partly because of the nightmares but also because he could never tell when he woke up whether that day was a school day or not. In the end he took a pencil and paper, and he drew a picture of a week, and could see that it had a good bump at each end — like a dog-bone. He then realized that all the little bits in the middle were the bits he didn't like — the school ones. When he counted these up there were only five, and the lumps at each end had two each, so he could see that there were four good days each week, and five bad ones. So he taught himself to hold his breath for the five bad ones, and this is how he survived.

It was good when he learned to draw a picture of the week, because then he could see what was real, and what was not real, and he didn't have to worry about things unless they were real. But it also meant that now he could see that Sunday night ended up on Monday morning, and school, and this made Sunday night the worst night of the week, the one when the nightmares were worst. Sometimes on these nights he would dream that he went to school in his pyjamas — but that was okay, because at least he had some clothes on. Often he dreamed that he had no pants on at all at school, and this meant he had to cover up his willy before anyone could see. Sometimes he even dreamed that he pooed himself at school, and he was always worried he was going to do a wet fart — and this wasn't even in a dream.

The pictures also were useful because they let him remember names — of people and of things. Just above his eyes, inside his head, there was a little TV screen. This is where he scrolls up the name of a person, maybe his brother, his sisters, his own name even, and if he can't get the name to come up on the screen, he can't read it, and so he can't remember it. And this happens often, and usually at the worst times, and then he has to try to describe with words what it is or who it is he is thinking about — and that makes people mad.

On one very fortunate day — because they now called him a 'retarded learner' — he was given a mother-help person 'to jolly him along'. She asked him to tell her what he had done in the weekend and was stunned by the huge volume of verbal information that this suddenly unleashed. He looked at the pictures in his head and started to talk. This resulted in Ernest's most satisfying and productive day at school, with a page and a half of written information produced before lunch. The message to his parents that afternoon shattered his joy when the teacher wrote that 'Ernest is obviously lazy, unmotivated and attention-seeking, and today's output proved that he is indeed an intelligent child manipulating the classroom situation to his own advantage.' He was never given mother-help again, and never really did figure out why there were words on that day but not on any other. But there were a lot of things that he didn't understand.

After this he would get very nervous at writing time and start to get so anxious that he would vomit. At other times the distress seemed to go the other way and he couldn't hold back the bad farts. Either result failed to impress the teacher and just added 'stinky stut' to the list of names they called him.

Later, much later as an adult, Ernest learned that those pictures in his head had yet another way of getting him into trouble — he was always accused of not listening. Ernest's dad wouldn't let any of the kids in the family have a cat or a dog, but for a short while he let them have some white mice as pets. These were kept in a cage, which the mice didn't like because they were trapped and couldn't run free, and he could feel how sad they were, just like him, longing for freedom.

Just how the conversation started slipped from Ernest's mind, but as an adult he can still hear his father's command before setting off to work — 'Don't take the mice out of the cage' — and he can still see equally clearly the picture the words put in his head at the time.

That evening, excited to talk to Dad, Ernest told him how he had shut all the doors in the hallway and let the mice run free for a while after school, and how they loved the space and the freedom, and were much happier when he put them back in the cage again.

After belting him with the leather strap, Dad sent Ernest to his bedroom to think about what he had done. Lying alone in the dark, his heart hurting more than his hand, Ernest asked God to take him home. 'I don't like this place, and I don't like being a people. Please God take me home.'

Many years later it gradually became apparent to Ernest that every time somebody said something to him that began with 'Don't' he got the wrong picture in his head and ended up doing the wrong thing. At first, he concluded that this must be because he was evil — church and Sunday School had taught him that some people are like this, and never obey — and that was why God wouldn't take him home.

Later when his brain got older and learned how to think usefully, he recognized that it is very hard to get a picture of 'Don't', and that when he was told 'Don't open the new honey pot', or 'Don't use the front door', the only picture he could get in his head was of the rest of the sentence, and he naturally remembered and followed the pictures in his head.

He even recognized that it was not his fault that he thinks in pictures, and that for years his parents and teachers were saying these things to him, hypnotizing him into doing the wrong thing. Really it hadn't been his fault at all, and it hadn't even really been their fault either, because nobody had told them that 'Don't' is not a useful word for kids who think in pictures. He dreamed that one day, if he ever got clever enough, he might write a book telling people what it was like to be an Ernest, so that mums, dads and teachers could do it differently.

Ernest had his own view on life, but he didn't know that it wasn't normal to look at things from any physical position you liked. He didn't know that other people didn't rise above the classroom like a bird and look down on what was going on. Or that other kids didn't sit inside the teacher's head and look out of her eyes as he often did. He didn't know that they couldn't see clearly how things would be if somebody did something differently, and all the things that would have happened in the alternative outcomes that followed, and he certainly didn't know that it was not normal to be able to remember the future, just like you could remember the past. This bit really annoyed him, because although he could often remember the future by getting a movie of it on the screen inside his head, he could never see his own stuff ahead of time, and he couldn't use this to keep himself out of trouble. It also puzzled him how other kids could tell the difference between what really happened in a situation, and all of the other things his head told him could have happened, and that he could see and remember so clearly in his mind. Their words, 'You're a liar, Stut', told him yet again that he had got it wrong.

One of the worst things that happened for Ernest was that every once in a while, maybe about one day in a hundred, he would have a 'good' day, and everything would go well. On these days his mouth would say the right things, he could sit and be just like the other kids, he could write his story so that the teacher could read it — and it made sense. When these days happened, he was so happy — until Dad and the teacher talked and they decided that they knew what was really going on. They knew that Ernest really was quite able to be like the other kids, and that most of the time he was just playing a stupid game. 'Attention-seeking', 'disruptive' and 'lazy' were the main words they used, and it just meant that they saw him as being bad. In the end, when he saw that he might be having a 'good' day, Ernest learned to tell the teacher that he felt sick and he would spend most of the day in the sick bay, avoiding doing the very thing he always longed to be able to do — doing well in class, just like the other kids.

Mat-time was horrible for Ernest. All the children had to sit on the floor in a big patch where they were all too close and in his space, and somebody would always be sitting on his shadow (or where his shadow would be), and although he couldn't find any pain there, he knew it was uncomfortable, and made him wriggle and be irritated. He couldn't tell the teacher that they were in his 'space' — she didn't understand and wouldn't listen, and always got annoyed with him. It would just have been easier if she had let him sit at the back so nobody was too close. Some kids were okay, though, because they sort of fitted in with him, but most of them were like sandpaper and being near them hurt.

It didn't help that his breath smelt bad and that he twitched his arms and legs constantly — sometimes even leaping right off the ground. It was his bad luck that the belief of the 1950s was that all children should drink milk — whether or not their individual digestive system could cope with it — and he innocently co-operated by becoming addicted to the stuff to the tune of four or five pints a day. This was also the time of other 'great food breakthroughs', and cordial and commercial fizzy drinks were beginning to wreak havoc with the nervous systems of sensitive children.

One of the things that he never learned to understand was why his brain would go tired, and he would yawn and feel groggy every time he had to read, write, do spelling or do maths. He never felt tired at art time or in 'phys-ed', at swimming time or at 'sport'. Playtime and lunchtime didn't bring the yawning, just all the stuff to do with words, the stuff that seemed to numb him and make him fall asleep.

As a product of all of this, Ernest felt bad about himself. He knew that nobody liked him, that God didn't care and that he was not a good person. When the headmaster told him off for not using a capital letter for his own name, Ernest looked into his eyes, and said that he didn't think he deserved a capital letter in front of his name — he wasn't good enough. Similarly, with his low self-concept ruling his behaviour, at the age of seven years he carried a broken arm for a full six weeks before finally telling his mother and asking for help.

Over time Ernest learned to become shy, to avoid putting himself at risk of rejection, and he learned to become a loner.

Later he found himself prone to exaggeration, trying to make things look good enough to be okay with other people, and as he grew into adulthood he found that his style carried the hallmark of people (mainly men) motivated by fear of rejection — he became a perfectionist, making sure that everything he did was beyond criticism, so that nobody could tell him that he was not good enough.

In his relationships with women, he showed a tendency to become 'co-dependent', trying desperately to please people, to be good enough, and to earn the acceptance and TLC that he had yearned for, for all those years through his childhood.

Eventually Ernest took up the challenge. He took writing tuition and sought help with elocution lessons and tips for public speaking. He went to university where he talked with the other students late into the night, picking their brains, because they had read the books. After seven years of study, he qualified as a psychologist with the specific aim of working with children, their teachers and their parents, so that some other kids could be spared a childhood like his.

Reaching the Reluctant Learner is the book he dreamed of writing.

Demystifying and legitimizing

In my first published writings in the early 1980s I opened the discussion of 'picture-thinking' as being the basis of common learning difficulties in the classroom. My exploration of the essence of dyslexia, Asperger's and autism then led me to develop the 'dual-brain continuum' as a pictorial model to help explain the 15 per cent of our students who somehow are not catered for adequately by our western education system (see Chapter Four).

Drawing on my early experience as a home mechanic, I then ventured the analogy of a *diesel* child sitting in a *gas/petrol* classroom, and by chance offered people on the autistic/Asperger's/dyslexia spectrum a new, clean descriptor — that of being a 'diesel' learner (see Chapter Four).

As well as legitimizing the pictorial, 'diesel' thinking/learning style, I also assert that this is not a learning difficulty, but a *legitimate* (albeit different) learning style, valid and valued, and of social significance as an enhanced problem-solving style.

Perhaps it is the teaching system that is in deficit, not the learner.

We have robbed society of a major positive, creative, contributing sector — simply because their style is practical and effective, rather than being intellectual and academic. In doing this we have promoted linguistic thinkers to the top of the social pile, and relegated non-linguistic thinkers to the status of 'also-ran'.

This book urges a revision of our implicit but unrecognized educational and social biases, and provides parents, teachers and others with a platform from which to work in their professional endeavours.

A life 'out of step'...

My personal contribution to the progressive dismantling of what is commonly called 'dyslexia' comes from my 70-plus years as a dyslexic person, and from 45 years as a psychologist working with children experiencing learning difficulties. My difficulties with reading have meant that I have not relied on the insights and conclusions of academics and scholars, but through observation of my own and others' learning processes have established my own understandings of what this unfortunately common difficulty is all about.

I am totally unapologetic that my understandings may differ from those of other 'experts' — some of whom have very evidently never been dyslexic for a single day of their life. To me their guesswork is evident.

All my life I have been 'out of step'. Being born just after the Second World War, this was the analogy to indicate being *unable to fit in*. I've never been part of the 'in group', I've never aspired to 'normal' values and objectives, and my thinking (when shared) has always seemed to raise eyebrows, hackles, resistance and tempers. In the end I learned to (sometimes) shut my mouth.

Looking back, I find it sad that I have had to live my life this way — but this is just one of the things that 'dyslexics' live with.

Did I choose to be dyslexic? Of course not. I was born this way! Who, in their right mind, would choose such a social and educational handicap? But then again, I know that my life is not an accident, and my belief is that I had a significant hand in designing its course and content. So if it is true that I wrote the script for this brief sojourn on the face of Planet Earth, then maybe I did choose my life, my style and my course.

If I did choose the setting dynamics of my life, it would make sense that I chose them for good purpose. In short, I believe that in writing the script for my life, I prescribed a series of childhood experiences that would allow and cause me to eventually write this book and offer these insights and understandings. If I had not lived the life, if I had not walked the walk, then I would be less able and less entitled to eventually talk the talk.

So is this task of my own choosing? In a way, yes, and in a way, no.

Somehow, by dint of fate or fortune I was born into a state where dyslexia saturated my daily life, and I have experienced dyslexia from every perspective, persistently. Its dynamics are in my bloodline, my DNA, and it is not a style that I would wish on anyone — at least until such time as our society and our educational system encompasses a useful understanding and acceptance of what dyslexia really is.

Not only will this take knowledge and insight, but a willingness to accept and implement this knowledge. And this is where my own role becomes apparent. My task as I see it, is to walk the interface between the non-dyslexics and the 'dyslexics', between the language thinkers and the pictorial thinkers — in my terms, between the 'petrols' and the 'diesels'.

In this I see two major functions. The first is to assist the parents and the teachers, the educational professionals and practitioners to understand what dyslexia really involves. Only when they can *see* what dyslexia involves from the perspective of the dyslexic will they be able to make the changes that will allow these 'diesel' children to succeed within our 'petrol' education system.

The second function is to present that same information in such a manner as to enable the dyslexic individual to begin to understand the dynamics of their own style. Once the 'diesel' understands that they have four wheels and a diesel motor, then they can comprehend and drive their vehicle of life. Otherwise, there is the danger that their misperception of themselves, the mistaken belief that they have shortcomings, will drive them — and drive them down.

Understanding our 'target group'

On a five-year seminar tour of New Zealand, I was informed by several school principals that 'No, we don't have any dyslexic students in this school' — with one going as far as to assert that there were no dyslexic students in his town!

Perhaps if the pupil is not doing well, they don't classify them as being a 'student', or perhaps (and more likely) if the child is 'performing poorly', or 'playing up', they are dismissed simply as having a 'poor attitude' or a 'poor background' rather than being dyslexic. Whatever the reason, it would seem that denial is still a real issue in some sections of education — with the extent of denial tending to increase with the age of the student group involved.

Although my five-year tour involved the presentation of over 500 seminars and workshops, it became apparent that the professional reception by schools would have been more positive if the presentation had been framed as 'Teacher Effectiveness Training', rather than the chosen descriptor, 'Dyslexia Dismantled'.

Two unsettling dynamics began to emerge:

- It became clear that there is still a significant stigma attached to the concept of dyslexia — a stigma that impacts on the person identified as dyslexic, and (of more concern) on the educational institution they attend.
- School-based Research and Training budgets are more likely to be targeted to improving teacher technique than to understanding the focus group of our teaching — in this case dyslexic children.

It is beyond debate that any successful marketing organization in any realm would acknowledge and comply with the simple baseline of 'First understand your target group'. Despite the obvious application to the educational setting, it would seem that there is little serious attempt to really explore and understand the processing style of the brain of the dyslexic child — both in and out of the classroom.

Towards understanding the bigger picture

That dyslexia is now getting more press, and more publicity, is a very positive development, with the hope that this will lead to more positive recognition of the needs of dyslexic children in our schools.

Hand in hand with this is the development of teaching programmes and 'apps' that are being made available to parents and schools, including remedial teachers in prisons, as the significance of dyslexia as a social dynamic is recognized.

As significant as this is, there is still an enormous gap in the literature and information that is available to parents and teachers. That gap involves the examination, focus and research of what dyslexia really is. What is it, where does it come from, who does it impact, how and why? Is it hereditary, perhaps a brain malfunction, a lack of some essential brain chemical, can it be remediated through medication?

Are we even clear as to what it involves, and how do we differentiate between dyslexia and other 'learning difficulties'? In some areas of the world, dyslexia and 'attention deficit disorder' are being lumped together and being generally referred to as 'ADD'. How are we to fairly and effectively respond if we are not even sure of what dyslexia really is? Is an observed difficulty with reading and writing a true and adequate definition of dyslexia, or is this rather obtuse malady rather a common representation, the tip of some larger, more insidious iceberg?

This book is not 'sexy' in that it does not offer fancy programmes or tricks to use to take the pressure off overloaded teachers in the classroom. Frequently I am asked to address teams of teachers, to give them techniques of how to deal with — or at least to be seen to be dealing with — dyslexia in the classroom.

I refuse. Rather I offer to present a four-hour workshop helping teachers to recognize dyslexia, where to look for it, indicators, characteristics so as to differentiate and recognize dyslexia as a specific impediment to successful teaching in the classroom. This, to me, is essential if we are to seriously assist the enormous section of our community who are currently offsided by our language-based education system.

I come to this task as a dyslexic person myself — as a reasonably bright student who suffered significant difficulty in my primary, secondary and tertiary educational history. Even now, some 50 years after finishing my formal education, my dyslexic tendencies still impact heavily on my daily life, as they do in the lives of many others who still struggle to make any sense of their own personal 'style'.

Learning or knowledge?

There is a significant difference between 'learning' and 'knowledge'.

'Learning', within the process of formal education, could be regarded as information gained from another person's experience — from observation, from being told, from being taught or from reading.

'Knowledge' could be argued to come from direct personal experience.

Both are subject to the process of interpretation, and neither can claim the status of implicit 'truth'.

The following story may serve to demonstrate the point:

In past years, education systems employed inspectors to assess and critique the standard of education being delivered by each and every teacher. These inspectors would visit schools, often with little warning, and sit in on classes — sometimes even interacting directly with the students to see what they had learned.

One such inspector ventured out of his city limits to visit a far-flung country school — a dyed-in-the-wool sheep-farming area — where it was rumoured that some farmers relied on the older children to assist with mustering, sometimes to the detriment of their formal schooling.

Taking a room in the local hotel, the inspector pondered a mechanism to strike an in-depth conversation with some of these young lads. From his upstairs room in the hotel, he surveyed stockyards across the road — the salesyards for the local farming community. 'Hit them on their home ground,' he thought.

Crossing the dusty road, he walked the perimeter of the yards, stopping along the railing to pluck the small tufts ripped from the animals' backs as they moved about the yards in the tension of the auction sales. With a collected fistful of natural fibre, he returned to his room to prepare for his ensuing inspection.

The next day, after briefly observing the class teacher in action, the inspector seized his moment, took charge of the class, and drawing the wool from his coat pocket held it up and asked, 'Can anybody tell me what this is?'

He paused, expecting a chorus of answers, or at least an array of hands, but was met with confused silence.

Recognizing a complete lack of confidence in these country kids, and realizing that they were probably shy and in awe of his city style, he coaxed them a little. 'Some of you will have seen this before ... It's okay to have a bit of a guess ... Somebody have a stab.'

Eventually a larger, possibly older boy rose from the rear of the room, asking to come forward to have a closer look. Taking the sample from the inspector, he hesitatingly ran it through his fingers, selected several pieces out, and held them up to the light.

'I'm not as sure as I'd like to be,' he started, 'but I'm picking that these bits here might be from the last of old Tom Watson's Perendale flock. This other lot has got to be a Southdown Cross of some sort, and as for this bit, well, some clown has gone and mixed it all with tail-hair off some drover's Border Collie mutt.'

There is an implicit difference between information that we have gleaned from educational exposure, and what we know from actual personal experience — knowledge.

The social environment — and being politically incorrect

When promoting change we need to be very aware of resistance, and of those who currently benefit from the status quo, and who may protest under the pain of possible loss.

Although it comes with huge social and personal costs attached, the dyslexic condition brings a certain convenience to some sections of our society. Our educational assessment system cuts a clean line between those who rate, and those who do not. Literacy and behavioural compliance are basic to being included in the group who rate, and (as a subsequent reading of this book will demonstrate) 'dyslexics' are at a specific disadvantage in both of these regards.

Struggling both in terms of literacy and behavioural compliance, the dyslexic can exercise far fewer positive choices in society and is in danger of becoming a social 'also ran'. As such they become grist for the mill in terms of the labour force, fiscal freedoms, personal health, advertising and social pressure — if you can't read or understand the small print, you are more likely to pay a high price in life. Sadly, we live in a society where the success of the successful is so often at the cost of the poor — the rich grow rich on the backs of the poor is an old adage, and it applies at a political, economic, administrative, legal and educational level.

Chapter Two
The nature of dyslexia

In this chapter I narrow the focus to get some clarity on the experience of being dyslexic, before presenting a series of snapshots, a range of guises and disguises that may mask the dyslexic condition.
- What is it like to be dyslexic?
- Hiding in plain sight: case presentations

What is it like to be dyslexic?

When people ask me this, I have to stop and think — because being dyslexic is normal for me, I've always been dyslexic, and I don't know any other way. Really, I suppose, I don't know what 'normal' is.

For years I thought I was 'normal' — although perhaps a little stupid, or maybe just 'dumb'. I knew I was always a little behind the eight ball, I didn't understand what the teacher was talking about, and couldn't 'pay attention' to the classroom situation — but with enough effort, huge concentration, and a degree of canny strategizing I got through.

Being dyslexic is usually associated with having reading and writing difficulties, and that is certainly the case for me. Eventually, somewhere round about my tenth birthday I figured I had mastered the art of 'reading' and became an avid reader — for the next three days. Finally, I gave up exhausted, having read my first book five or six times — up to page six — and eventually realizing that although I could read and say each word, I had no idea what they meant or what the book was about. Now, as an adult I will happily dig your garden or mow your lawn in preference to reading a book. The notion of a soft armchair and a 'good book' is one of sheer torture for me.

Really, dyslexia is about language, and about not being able to do language well. Difficulty with 'reading' is only one part of being dyslexic — but let's explore that for a moment.

As a dyslexic, I know that words are the things that come out of your mouth — and into your ears. The things in books, or in the newspaper, are not really words at all; they are just pictures of words, they are things to remind you of the words that you can say, hear and think. The really hard part is that they are made up of squiggles, black marks on white paper — and these things have no recognizable resemblance to anything real at all, and especially not to whatever it is that they are meant to be referring to.

What I mean is, whereas I understand that the Chinese symbol for 'mountain' actually looks like a mountain, in our language the squiggles called 'letters' bear no similarity to a high hill at all. This might not be a problem to you, but I'm dyslexic, and that means that *I think in pictures*, and with these 'letter' things, I don't get the picture at all.

I don't know what most people see when they open a book, but the first thing I see is flashes of lightning jumping all over the page. When my primary school teacher asked what I meant, I drew a line where the lightning went, and she said that it followed the gaps between the words down the page. I said, 'Yes, this is the same as the snake in Snakes and Ladders, and my eyes always slide to the bottom.'

The same teacher asked me why I like to draw a line around my page, and I told her it is not a line, but a fence — like on a farm — to stop the words, and my eyes, from wandering off the page. (The border on the pages of this book is designed to be similarly helpful to dyslexic readers.) I was not allowed to draw my lines on school reading books, and that made reading too hard. The words wouldn't stay still long enough for me to work them out, and they kept jumping from one place to another. The teacher put a blank card under the line I was reading, and that helped — but they wouldn't let me do it at college.

Now as an adult with my laptop I can finally write (neatly what's more) because the computer puts all the bits in the right place, the letters and the words in the right order. I know that these days I can get a computer to read out loud for me, but the interesting thing is, cartoon strips work really well for me, because all the pictures are there and I can see exactly what the message is. I can even 'read' the words in cartoon strips — and this is because they are all in square letters or capitals, which people like me find easier to understand.

What about 'writing' for the dyslexic?

Yes, this is hard too. The first reason is because 'writing' always seems to involve words — but that is obvious. What is not obvious is that to write words you first have to choose words to write. What if you don't have any words in your head? Yes, I have plenty of ideas, memories, fantasies and creations — but I *see* them, in pictures, and I cannot readily find words to represent them. In my head my internal video screen might show a pack of frenzied chihuahuas terrorizing the police in the city, and I write on my page 'The little dogs...' then give up in disgust and frustration.

The other main reason for writing being hard has got something to do with our tendency to carry what I call a 'residual left-handed-orientation'. 'Normal' people often don't realize that most tools are designed for right-handers (most of our population), and they don't really suit left-handers. But more than this, they certainly don't realize that this is also the case with the letters of the alphabet, and with the direction we read and write in — which is all designed for right-handers. Apparently, the Phoenicians designed all this, with no consideration for the lefties in the population. I'm not saying that all 'dyslexics' are left-handed or that all left-handers are dyslexic, but most 'dyslexics' that I have met can quickly identify a left-hander in their immediate family tree. And that doesn't include our elders who, as children, were changed from left to right by well-intentioned educators!

Being a lefty isn't so bad in itself these days, except that lefties naturally go from right to left across the page, and we naturally draw our circles in a clockwise direction — and this is in reverse from what our reading system demands. My point is that we spend all our educational life having to do our reading and writing in reverse gear. Great.

So what is it like to be dyslexic?

Well, we think in pictures, we chase words around the pages of books, and we have trouble finding any sensible connection between squiggles on paper and real things they are meant to refer to. And this all happens in perpetual reverse gear. You guessed it, for us, school is not cool, and for most of us this makes life tough.

So you think in pictures?

Yes, I think in pictures. You say 'dog', and I get a picture of a dog in my head. You probably do the same — and that doesn't make you dyslexic. You say 'fiction' and you probably know what it means, but I just look at you strangely because I can't get a picture of that word. I can't draw a simple picture of what it means. I also can't get a picture of 'respect', or 'tidy', or 'behave' or lots of other words that parents and teachers use, so I have only a very hazy idea of what these words might mean — but parents and teachers keep asking children to do these things. They probably don't realize how hard this is for the children — who really do want to please them. Unfortunately, the parents won't or can't understand, and they just think the child is being uncooperative.

I'll explain examples of this like 'hurry up', and 'come here' later in this book.

So dyslexia affects behaviour too?

Yes, it affects behaviour too. I often don't understand instruction or what people want of me. They know what they mean, but the words make no sense to me. It's even worse when they say 'Don't ...' then put a picture of me doing something in my head. They do this with 'Don't slam the door', and 'Don't spill your drink', 'Don't be late' and lots of other hypnotic commands. When I comply with the pictures they give me, I get the blame, and I am told that I am bad and a troublemaker. I see that there is no picture for 'Don't' — can you see this? Can you understand that they blame the child for not following their instruction, when the child is doing the best they can? Really it would be better if they told the child *what they do want* — not what they don't want.

Most people think in words, but 'dyslexics' think in pictures. This is a bit like petrol (words) and diesel (pictures). I go to school and the nice teacher-lady puts petrol in my diesel tank, and I can't make it work — I can't learn and I can't co-operate … but I get the blame.

Back to the question: What is it like to be dyslexic?

What goes on inside my head? What do I think? Do I think? Really the answer has to be 'No'. I'm not really sure what 'think' means. You have a petrol brain that uses words to think with. In my head there aren't any words, and there aren't really any thoughts. I have eyes inside my head that have lots of pictures going through them, like lots of videos, all at once. Some of these are now, some are from the past — and some are from the future, all at once. Some are 'true' and some of them I create, but I can't tell one from the other; they all look the same. You say I have a good fantasy and a good memory, but really this is only for pictures. Have you ever stopped to look at what the word *'imagination'* really means? Yes, *image thinking.*

When someone asks me what I am thinking I can't answer. The first reason I can't answer is that I can see about 6000 things in my videos at any one moment — so which bit shall I talk about? It is easier to just shrug my shoulders and say, 'Nothing.' The second reason is that there are just pictures in my head — and feelings. 'Telling you' means using words, and I'm not good at that. I often end up wanting to share but can't find the words — or use lots of wrong words, or far too many words, too fast. It's not a great way to make friends.

The worst is when I say words, and people hear them, but I used the wrong words that don't say what I mean. But people say that that is what I said, so it must be what I meant. More than this, can

I ask you, please, please don't ask me how I feel — that is just too hard. This is why I shrug my shoulders so often.

And while I'm on the subject, when you want me to learn something, or to understand something, telling me with words is not the best way to go. *Show me*, walk me through it, and I will have a far better chance of understanding and giving you what you want.

So to answer your question 'What is it like to be dyslexic?

It is like always getting it wrong. Being 'bad' when you are trying to be good. Being always in the dark and thinking that you must be dumb and stupid. Finding things hard when you are told that they are easy. Like working yourself to exhaustion, then being told you are not trying hard enough. Like wanting to please your parents and teachers, but just making them angry. Like being unable to share your ideas usefully with other people, and of not even knowing how you feel. Like being too scared to try, because you know it will only lead to failure — again. Like living a daily nightmare where everything is out of control, and being too scared to sleep at night because of the horrendous nightmares that haunt you under cover of darkness. The anxiety, the fear and the insecurity are horrendous — they are overpowering and depressing, and they don't go away, even when you get older. The feeling of 'not being good enough' never goes away, and medication does not help.

Thank you for your questions, and for your interest, but I almost wish you hadn't asked.

As interesting and insightful as it may be, this information above is the 'inside story', and yet doesn't help us much to identify our elusive dyslexic. How does he present himself, and what does he do?

The remaining part of this chapter looks at a range of 'presentations' — guises and disguises — that may help us in our endeavour to unmask dyslexia.

Hiding in plain sight: case presentations

It has been said that the only consistent thing about dyslexia is its inconsistency, with symptoms and presentations differing widely from one person to the next. Characteristics will mix with traits unpredictably, with the result that what is a difficulty for one person with dyslexia may be a specific talent for another. A highly coordinated sportsperson, presenting an intuitive predictive skill, may be just as dyslexic as another who may have a combination of dyspraxic traits (clumsiness), lack depth perception and eye–hand coordination — but emerge as a creative chef.

Yes, as inferred earlier, dyslexia is a master of camouflage. The following presentations, selected from a casebook spanning 45 years, are included here to assist in identification, and as a demonstration of some of the less recognizable jigsaw portraits encountered over my career. These case presentations are just a few classic demonstrations of the way that dyslexia can present in a person's educational, medical or mental-health life, but not be recognized by family, friends or experts. It has long been apparent to me that the predominance of referrals to my office by medical practitioners — for depression, schizophrenia, bipolar and 'personality disorders' — are in fact of people who, in one form or another, are battling the effects of undiagnosed dyslexia.

Framing has long been used in art to draw the attention of the eye to what the artist has selected as the subject matter of the piece, and to equally draw the eye away from all the distractions of the immediate environment. So, too, this book is designed and written as a framing exercise. It is designed to draw the perception away from confusing distractors (and mislabelling) and to assist both parents and professional operators to see, to recognize and to focus on the dynamics that are central to catering sensitively to the needs of the dyslexic person — be they adult or child.

Thus, our initial focus will be on framing distractors out so as to facilitate better recognition of dyslexic characteristics when they are presented to us — sometimes under heavy disguise.

Although over recent years I have personally presented over 500 two-and-a-half-hour seminars on dyslexia around New Zealand, very few children or adults are actually referred to me as being recognized 'dyslexics'.

A disproportionate number of my clients are referred around the age of seven to ten years, generally because they are bedwetters, or they have tried or are threatening suicide. Lack of academic achievement and the related anger, frustration and behavioural difficulties don't appear to warrant seeking help — almost as if they are deemed to fall within the parameters of what is considered to be normal elements of childhood.

I am convinced that dyslexia is misunderstood by the public and professionals alike, and it certainly seems to be the case that few within the helping agencies have any direct personal experience of what it may involve.

It always strikes me as ironic that the self-proclaimed experts in this field are predictably highly qualified academics whose implicit skill with language, and linguistic processing, is a natural barrier to their being able to have any real understanding of the dyslexic reality.

In my experience it is important for both the family and the child's class teacher to understand what dyslexia really is, the forms it can take, and the real mixture of ways it can present. However, over and above this, it is imperative that the growing child should be able to get a cumulative understanding of their own style — so that they can learn to live with it, accommodate it, and utilize it to their advantage.

In 40 years of my private practice and government employment, certain consistencies became apparent in the way some of my clients presented. The clients sampled below all demonstrated the presence of dyslexia that had not been identified by teachers, social workers, family doctors, psychologists or psychiatrists they had previously consulted.

These brief case outlines (names have been altered for anonymity) are included here to demonstrate to the reader the myriad presentations that dyslexia can take — so as to better enhance the general recognition and identification of dyslexia in the general population and in particular in children.

Without identification, many of the Ernests of the world drop out of education, become lifelong victims of bullying, and some even drop out of life. Some practise the role of 'social misfit', others become antisocial in a life of drugs or crime, and yet others absent themselves through suicide. Many do manage to successfully stay afloat in life, but at the cost of being heavily impacted by the winds and currents of social pressure.

If we are to be at all supportive of any of these people, we need to be sure that we have a clear understanding of who they are.

Jeremy

Jeremy, aged seven years, was referred as a very bright, depressed, angry and confrontative child who had attempted suicide several times. Although he was achieving satisfactorily in his school work, to me he was clearly dyslexic, but this had not been considered by any of the range of agencies to whom he had previously been referred. The fact that he was obviously highly intelligent but equally confrontative had earned him a range of diagnoses, but not that of dyslexia.

It is still commonly assumed that if a person is obviously intelligent, or if they appear to be able to read and write, by definition they cannot be dyslexic. First, dyslexia is not in any way related to intelligence levels, despite the fact that some authorities argue that 'dyslexics' are generally 'highly intelligent'. Dyslexic people have a different way of thinking, but this does not make them more or less intelligent. Second, although their dyslexia may mean that some people find reading or writing (or both) or number skills to be extremely difficult to master, others may eventually learn some mastery in these skills.

Jeremy's major presenting problem was that when told *not* to do something, he would immediately defiantly do it.

Jeremy himself explained: 'When my mummy or my daddy or my teacher tells me not to do something, I go and do it straight away. I know I shouldn't, but I just do. I know I am evil, and I should be dead.'

One psychologist dubbed this 'oppositional defiant disorder' (ODD), suggesting that Jeremy's behaviour was based in anger and defiance. However, his family doctor had dubbed it 'auditory processing disorder' (APD), suggesting that Jeremy thought *don't* means *do*. Another specialist identified it as 'cognitive processing disorder' (CPD), suggesting the behaviour indicates a particular processing deficiency, where the brain doesn't 'hear' the *don't* part of the command.

I saw it as a product of dyslexia and focused my attention on the parenting style used by his mum and dad, rather than focusing on Jeremy.

In discussion with his parents, I ascertained that their parenting style included the common style of putting most instruction in the negative form. This involved saying things like 'Don't leave your bag there', instead of saying 'Put your bag in your bedroom' or 'Don't slam the door' instead of 'Shut the door gently'.

A small change in their language style where they no longer told him what *not* to do, but rather used pictorial language indicating what they *did want* him to do, quickly changed the visual imagery in his memory, and thereby what he consequently did. This had a direct and positive impact on the lives of everybody in the family, and the miserable depressed child morphed into a happy loving lad.

Mitchell

Mitchell was a very angry thirteen-year-old who lived on the street after running away from a very violent father. He related far better to wild dogs than to social workers, and he could not be contained in welfare facilities. A natural survivor, he had learned not to trust adults — especially those who claimed to 'care'.

'Behaviour Change' programmes only drove Mitchell to more extreme antisocial reactions, and to an even closer bond with his canine counterparts. However, when communicated with according to classic dyslexic style, he emotionally collapsed and responded like the desperately sad and lonely child that he really was.

Mitchell had been placed in nine welfare homes before I met him. Some of his caregivers believed that all they needed to do was 'give him love'. Others put their faith in behaviouristic 'reward and punishment' approaches. Mitchell had experienced too much violence, manipulation and bullying in his early life to tolerate these approaches, and to him 'nice people' were just covering unrealistic expectations, and he knew that their thinly covered 'not nice' sides were just waiting to pounce. He had also discovered that dogs are one of the very few animals that come close to being truly unconditional in their love — and he had a natural communication with dogs, so this is where he focused his positive emotions.

In my experience, dyslexic boys appreciate communication that they recognize as being direct, honest and not tainted by manipulation or leverage of any sort. I simply told him he had no reason to trust me, to be on his guard in case I had any expectations of him, but that if he chose I would work with him — because I was being paid to. He would need to choose any goals to work toward, and, if I agreed with those goals, I would support him. He was the boss.

We worked together on a fortnightly basis for about 18 months until he finished school and joined the workforce. He continued to visit me at my home (with dog attached) long after he graduated from his 'welfare' status.

Jesse

Jesse, an intelligent and overtly sensitive lad, arrived at my office with his father. He had recently left school and had secured an apprenticeship in plumbing — because 'he is good with his hands'. His mother had insisted that he stay on at school until the age of seventeen, despite his misery and almost total lack of success.

His teachers had consistently assured her that they knew he was bright, and that 'he would soon come right'.

His recurring panic attacks were pushing him to consider suicide, prompting his father to email me for an appointment. Jesse was stunned when I opened the interview by asking him how many left-handers there were in his family (three) and asking him if he was aware that he is classically dyslexic.

By the end of the four-hour session his father acknowledged that he was now aware that he too was dyslexic along with both Jesse's sister and brother. None had previously been diagnosed as such.

Many class teachers dismiss dyslexia as a possibility because they recognize that the student is overtly intelligent. This assumption that a person can't be dyslexic if they are obviously intelligent often sits alongside another assumption which links 'naughty' behaviour with being dull and undisciplined.

There is still a strong belief in the completely irrational notion that children who are failing in class and have behaviour problems are simply 'acting out' and 'attention-seeking'. In many cases these are responses to negative verbal instruction (e.g. 'No running around the swimming pool' — which induces a visual image of running around the pool, which in turn has an almost hypnotic impact on the dyslexic child, creating the behaviour which earns the child the 'naughty' label), and to physical, mental and emotional exhaustion from the constant strain of trying to interpret and make sense of spoken language so as to avoid being seen as being 'naughty'.

I have seldom met a child who actually desired to be rejected by parents or teachers, and few children find value in being the target of punishment. Yet parents and teachers cling to the belief that children choose this outcome. Similarly, I can find no value in the throwaway comment that a child is 'attention-seeking'. However, it does make full sense to me that the child might have exhausted their emotional, mental and physical fuel supplies and is 'energy seeking', desperately seeking a response, any response, where an adult may glare at them, yell at them or even touch them, and in doing so inject a little energy into the child's flat batteries.

If we see and label the child as 'attention-seeking', we commonly follow up with the notion 'don't pay them any attention — ignore them'. This will leave the child in their exhausted state and (as the behaviourists tell us) the child's behaviour will get worse as their desperation increases! However, if we allow ourselves the sensitivity of recognizing the child's dyslexic plight — their confusion, fear, stress, anxiety and exhaustion — we may choose to react differently and work *with* the child rather than against them.

Georgina

Georgina (fourteen) was referred by her family doctor for depression and for 'disengagement' in the classroom. An enlightened practitioner, her GP had refused Georgie's mother's request for antidepressant medication on the grounds that there must be some reason for the depression, and that she was too young to be subjected to medication and all the predictable downstream repercussions. (It is important for us to consider that 'depression' is not an illness in itself but is rather a symptom of a personal state. When we take antidepressants, we are not addressing the situation that is making us feel depressed, but rather just using chemicals to dull the feelings around the situation.)

Georgie was a very intelligent young woman who was acutely observant and was highly sensitive to what she observed. Although Georgie's father appeared to be a right-hander, his own mother acknowledged that she had worked hard when he was very young to stop him using his (natural) left hand. As a very bright young man he had accommodated the stresses that this incurred, and as an adult had no notion that he was naturally left-handed. Georgie's mother was naturally right-handed, and Georgie considered herself a natural right-hander as well.

She was, however, just slightly 'different'. Her eye–hand coordination was poor, so she was regarded by others as 'clumsy'. Similarly, her body coordination was affected, she walked without grace, and found dancing and rhythmic movement difficult. In her social interactions she preferred meaningful discussion and found the 'chat' of her peers petty and empty. In short, she did not socialize well with her peers but preferred to interact either with people much older than herself or much younger.

Georgie was very bright and perceptive, and she saw very clearly that she was different from most people her age. Like most 'dyslexics' I have worked with she felt her differences were negative, but she could not overcome them and be or act like other kids. She felt her only recourse was to 'become like a snail, withdraw into my shell, and hide from exposure to the rest of the world'. Like most depressed people I have worked with, Georgie was unable to achieve the things, the goals that mattered most to her. All her efforts to be like other people ended in disaster, usually being teased — and sometimes bullied — about her clumsy efforts. She became a social isolate.

In her withdrawal Georgie had become an astute observer of human behaviour and had gained quite an understanding of the role of fear as a prime social motivator — and was eventually able to see this in her own situation as well as that of others. Georgie's greatest need from me was an insightful understanding of her own style — her version of dyslexia — a predominantly right-sided person with a wee smattering of 'left' from her loving father.

I eventually lost contact with her when she left town to do a BA in Psychology.

Peter

Peter, aged seven, had evidently been absolutely miserable from his first day at school. His teacher reported to me that he was 'poorly socialized', and that he would not play with other children. He refused to do any form of homework and would put no effort into any classroom learning. She indicated that she had virtually given up on him and found it easiest to let him opt out at the back of the class. Despite all this, she had not communicated any of this detail to the parents but just reported to them that he presented no problem at school.

Peter's parents, busy developing their own professional lives, did not recognize that anything was amiss until one evening his mother drove her car into the garage to find him standing on a chair with a noose around his neck. In an interview, both parents recognized major similarities in their own school history, but neither had any notion that they both suffered a lifetime of difficulties directly related to what is now recognized as being dyslexic.

Although both presented as being intelligent, neither had done well at school, and both acknowledged that 'everything in life is an uphill battle'.

In our subsequent work both parents acknowledged being personally motivated by an overt fear of failure, and they had consequently become 'compulsive achievers'.

The greatest difficulty associated with dyslexia is the task of 'making sense of language'. Whereas most people have their predominant intellectual functioning centred in their language brain (for ease we refer to this as being the left frontal hemisphere), the dyslexic person, by nature, processes information and 'thinks' using their pictorial, image-based brain — in the right frontal hemisphere — in their imagination. Language-based thinkers hear or read a language-based message, process it in their linguistic brain, and respond to it from there. The dyslexic person, however, has about five times as much processing to do in order to understand or respond to verbal information. They hear or read the message with their language-based brain, but then in order to process and make sense of it they have to transfer it to their pictorial brain so that they can 'see' what the message means. If the message is pictorial (The boat is red) this is a simple matter, but if the message has no pictorial component (The situation was remarkable) or has ambiguous pictorial content (The old man slept like a log) extra processing is required and degrees of confusion are probable. The dyslexic person is likely to be seen as 'a slow thinker', as being 'a bit dull', as 'not being with it', and is likely to withdraw in their confusion, and in their fear of being seen to be inadequate. They may become a social isolate or the butt of teasing and bullying by peers.

Hence, we see increasing levels of disengagement as children go through school, finally withdrawing altogether, with the possibility of becoming socially marginalized.

Tui

Tui, at age eleven was referred to me in my role as Education Psychologist, but he would never have been referred to me as a private practitioner. I discovered that Tui was referred only as a product of pressure from the parents of other children at his school, because of his persistent bullying. He was branded 'the worst kid in the school — big, aggressive, disobedient and a bully'.

However, when I took Tui aside for some one-to-one assessment, I met a pleasant, intelligent, left-handed and frustrated child who was in my opinion being bullied by an insensitive teacher in an intolerant system. The teacher was not at all interested in the difficulties Tui was experiencing in the learning environment and would not accept my diagnosis that he was dyslexic.

His mother was a warm, intelligent and loving woman who was deeply hurt by the overt racism she and her family experienced at the school. His father, who himself had had difficulties at school, was determined that Tui would not fail, so he had resorted to overly strong methods to ensure Tui's school success — including (with the teacher's support) forcing him to change to be a right-hander! I began to see Tui's 'bullying' behaviour as being his response to an almost complete loss of personal power.

A change of handedness (back to his left hand), together with a change of teacher at school, allowed a more tolerant and supportive approach to be implemented in the classroom. This was rewarded by an almost explosive leap in his academic learning, his social relationships, and his constructive role within the school community. Within months he was voted by other students as 'class captain' and was achieving happily in his academic work with spectacular success in his 'art and creativity'.

Jed

Jed (42) was resistant, grumpy and confused when he bumbled into my office one morning. He had been given an ultimatum by his wife of twelve years: 'Get some help or I am out of here.' She was sick of his unpredictable moodiness, his unwillingness (or inability) to communicate, and his perpetual style of starting projects but never finishing them.

Apparently, Jed was a very creative, even artistic, guy, capable and talented in a wide range of activities, but his perfectionist tendencies and low 'self-concept' got in the way of any real achievement. His wife had had enough and wanted positive change or at least some decent explanation of his frustrating style.

In a word, Jed was dyslexic. He had always known that he was creative and talented, but his track record at school had convinced him that he was also 'dumb and stupid'. He cited many instances of teacher put-downs to support this notion.

A 'cause and effect' chain was evident; Jed had been told that he was stupid — the evidence from his schooling reinforced the notion — and he had lived his life accordingly. His adult life demonstrated a classic fear of failure (therefore an unwillingness to invest his energies in a serious way), as well as a clear fear of 'success' (because if he succeeded in doing something, he would be expected to be able to do it again — and it doesn't always work that way with dyslexia). He also seemed to have unconsciously recognized that appraisal of a person's output happens when the task is completed, so he was safe from evaluative criticism if he never actually finished his projects.

Gordon

Gordon, aged sixteen, was still at school, but simply because there was nothing else that he thought he could do. Gordon told me that he knew he was 'dumb' because he could not understand language. He could hear what people said, and he could even repeat accurately what he had heard them say. But much of the time he could not make any sense of the words and language that he had heard. Similarly, he could read (at a basic level), but the words were usually just black squiggles on white paper and gave him no meaning. Even when he could read them aloud, they were just sounds without sense or significance.

Through most of his school life he used cunning tricks to disguise his difficulties, and basically 'seduced' his teachers with his spontaneity, his 'gift of the gab', and by being expressly polite and helpful. He had the advantage of being good looking, and of being a natural athlete, and 'scored' in both regards. He was very excited to discover and explore the intricacies of dyslexia as it applied to him, and after leaving school he found particular success in acting and stand-up comedy with the support and assistance of a particularly accepting girlfriend.

Bruce

Bruce was referred to me by his accountant. A welder by trade, Bruce was otherwise uncertificated but was more creative, artistic and ingenious than any engineer I had previously encountered. Bruce's problem was that he wasn't able to run a business.

His fear of failure meant that he was an absolute perfectionist, that he spent excessive time on each job, but only invoiced customers for a fraction of the time spent. He was well known in the wider community for his work, but also for the fact that his fear of displeasing his customers meant that bad debts were never followed up. Bruce had a thriving business but was horrifically poor and was going under.

We very quickly established that Bruce had virtually nil reading and writing ability, that all his interactions were via word of mouth, and that as a consequence he was forced to trust other people's honesty and integrity in all his interactions — to his inevitable detriment. Anger and depression were mounting, and he was turning to drugs and alcohol as a result.

Many 'dyslexics' are extremely creative and are gifted problem-solvers. In their mind's eye they see the finished product in absolute detail before they have even begun, then sequentially problem-solve its creation from beginning to end through every meticulous perfected detail. Unfortunately, this giftedness has a price: the fact that they can never charge for the huge amount of time and energy they have invested in the product.

Jared

Jared, a young man with a wide smile, gently cradling a tiny baby in his arms, accosted me in my local supermarket. Turning to his equally young wife, he loudly announced, 'This man saved my life.'

Twenty years earlier Jared had been referred to me at the age of five by a local welfare agency after he lit a fire under the cot where his infant sister was quietly sleeping. On a previous occasion he had crawled under the family home and kindled a fire there — and demonstrated huge pride regarding his knowledge and ability to do this. Although his mother went to considerable lengths to hide the one packet of matches she kept in the house, Jared could always sniff them out within minutes.

His school teacher described him as being 'genuinely hyperactive' and pointed to him sitting atop a cupboard two and a half metres high, announcing, 'He just shimmied up the vertical side of that cupboard.'

Jared had been labelled as having attention-deficit/hyperactivity disorder (ADHD), and although he is still the only child I have met in many years of practice that I would agree was truly hyperactive, I did not agree for one moment that he had an 'attention deficit'. One look at his face and the quick movements of his eyes told me that this child took notice of everything.

It is a standard situation that our senses are bombarded with a huge amount of input at any given moment. It is also normal that we develop a protective ability to filter much of this input out so that our cognition is not constantly overloaded. But some children do not seem to have acquired this defence system.

Although ADD may be an apt description for what the observer thinks they can see from the outside, the reality of the situation is that the so-called ADD child is paying attention to *absolutely everything* — their system is being totally bombarded by stimuli from all their senses and the child ends up bouncing off the walls like a demented possum trapped in a broom cupboard.

Although a local psychiatrist had recommended that Jared be put on Ritalin, his mother stood her ground, recognizing that putting foreign chemicals into his brain would be more likely to poison him than remedy the situation.

It turned out that Jared's father had been a smooth-talking travelling musician who could play every musical instrument but couldn't settle long enough to parent the children he fathered — and that Jared had no obvious hand dominance, being neither left nor right-handed.

Working with his teacher, I used an old refrigerator packing crate to minimize some of the stimuli Jared was having to cope with in the classroom, along with ear muffs, and very constrained expectations of his concentration span. I supported Jared through ten years of schooling, never really feeling that I was doing justice to his needs, then lost contact when he finally escaped the clutches of the education system. Until meeting him again in the supermarket...

Francis

Francis was just six years old when he was referred with a stutter that was almost a complete block to any effective speech at all. In the school setting he could manage only a few single words, each the product of nine or ten attempts, and certainly no sentences. It was as if his tongue was in full mutiny. At home, with sufficient effort he could manage to make himself understood but, surprisingly, at his nana's house he was virtually fluent.

His previous speech and language therapist reported that Francis had begun to develop quite normal speech at the appropriate age, but on the death of his much-loved grandfather the stutter had taken hold, and all her approaches to remedy the problem via speech therapy had been in vain. She understandably concluded that the problem was a deep-seated emotional issue and referred the lad to my office.

After observing Francis at school (but refraining from attempting to engage him) I visited his home to obtain permission to observe him at his nana's house.

Here he was relaxed and at ease and happily shared his train set with me. I noted that in his play activities he was favouring left-handedness, but his body posture suggested that he was right-eye dominant. Casual checking under the guise of play quickly revealed that he was consistently right-footed and right-eyed, but distinctly left-handed.

Such a mixture is not unusual in itself, but in my experience it was not likely to be sufficient to create his extraordinary stutter — especially after the successful establishment of normal speech.

While pursuing a full and complete case-history I discovered that Francis had always been a very agile and active lad, with a penchant for heights. Just before his fifth birthday he had fallen from an apple tree while chasing an elusive fruit. The fall left him with a badly broken right arm and an obligatory plaster cast that he wore over the major part of the summer and his initial school months in the new year. When the cast eventually came off, his climbing adventures began again — resulting in a gentle slide down the garage roof with an abrupt landing on the lawn below — with the same arm well and truly broken again.

In all, Francis had his right (normally dominant) arm in a plaster cast for the first eight months of his school life. With his right arm and hand essentially out of action, Francis had learned to become a left-hander — and now wrote with his non-dominant left hand. By chance this had coincided with the death of his much-loved grandfather, and the onset of the stutter.

Our response to this situation was really surprisingly simple. We took his left hand out of operation. No, not by breaking his arm, but by disabling his left pincer-grip with a carpenter's fingerstall. This leather thumb protector nicely contained the little boy's thumb and first finger, meaning that any hand operation using the finger and thumb had to be done with his right hand — his natural dominant hand.

Over a period of weeks Francis's natural right-handedness was re-established, and his stutter vanished within two weeks.

By way of explanation, I can only muse that it is possible that the muscles that are responsible for speech are the most emotionally labile of the human body and can present as an indicator of laterality issues.

Jonathon

Jonathon was at a tipping point and needed to make a decision. At age 28 he had spent much of his adult life in and out of prison. He was cynical and untrusting and had learned to survive as a petty criminal. He was very evidently not happy with his way of life, but it worked for him and he knew no other.

His real difficulty came when he met and fell in love with a truly lovely woman who wished better for him. There is truth in the old saying that when a man meets a woman he wants her to stay as she is forever. But when a woman meets a man she can see the potential beyond his current self, and she wants him to achieve that potential.

Sheila loved what she saw — but what she saw was what she wanted him to become — and for the first time in his life Jonathon wanted to please somebody other than himself.

I include reference to Jonathon's case, not because of how I worked with him, but rather to make the point that apparently 64 per cent of the New Zealand prison population is left-handed — and that 84 per cent are deemed to be dyslexic.

I can't vouch for the accuracy of those figures, but my experience with prisons, prisoners and ex-prisoners suggests that the rates are probably this high in most 'developed' countries of the world. It is common knowledge that the literacy rate of the prison population of most western societies is extremely low, but that inmates who learn to read and write while 'inside' are less likely to reoffend.

With low rates of literacy, they will also have low rates of formal qualifications. This means they will generally be on lower wages than average, with less job security — but of course they still have the same aspirations as other people — they still want the goodies that money can buy. So they cheat, get caught and go to prison.

A more insightful approach at primary-school level might save them, and the greater society, an awful lot of hassle.

Pierre

Pierre was a classroom wanderer, and at the age of eight he was referred for help on the basis of behaviour suggesting that he was habitually procrastinating. Either that or he was overtly lazy and intent on avoiding any active involvement in classwork.

I observed Pierre in class after the teacher had instructed the children to 'Carry on with the project work you began yesterday'.

Pierre walked around the classroom looking at what other individual children were doing for some time, then moved to a pile of 'resource books', where he started leafing through books on an apparently random basis.

After fifteen minutes or so I asked him to tell me about his project. He responded immediately with evident interest in his chosen topic — a particular dinosaur he had seen pictured in a book but could not name. His knowledge of the particular beast was impressive, yet he could not remember its name nor what book he had seen a picture of it in.

Pierre was evidently quite confused and embarrassed about his memory difficulty, so he was desperately searching, hoping to stumble on the book, the picture, the name, so that he could get into his project.

His conversation indicated that he was not aware that other children in his class had the benefit of a linguistic memory that gave them entry into their projects, and the tools to process the information involved. He inferred that he sometimes wondered how others knew what to do, and where to find the information — yet he did not.

His evident linguistic deficit was my first clue to his right-brain dominance and the real source of his 'reluctant involvement'.

The new farm cadet

It was early Monday morning and they suddenly appeared at my office door. No appointment, no phone call, no warning. He was big, an outdoors man, and grumpy to say the least. He shoved a very timid fifteen-year-old lad in through my open door and demanded 'You a psychologist? Then fix him!'

On invitation the farmer told his story.

The lad was his new farm cadet, released early from school to gain practical knowledge of farming. A great scheme, when it works.

On the previous evening the farmer and the lad were in the cowshed milking. The milking was nicely under way and the farmer instructed the lad: 'Get on the quad bike. Go up the cattle-race. Don't open the gate by the cattle-stop, open the next one.' Good clear communication. Well, maybe not.

After the milking, the lad shut the gate again, and the day's work was done.

Early the next morning the farmer got on the quad bike and went up the race to get the cows — and discovered the herd of 200 animals happily grazing on a 30-acre paddock of standing hay. The boy had opened the gate by the cattle-stop, and the destruction of a significant portion of the predicted annual farm income was complete.

What happened here?

The boy was not at all academic and had left school early for a farming job. This strongly suggested a dyslexic style, which I later confirmed.

Being a pictorial thinker, he listened to and processed the boss's instructions:

'Get on the quad bike.' (Visualizes self on quad.)

'Go up the cattle-race.' (Visualizes the race.)

'Don't open the gate by the cattle-stop. (As there is no pictorial component to the word 'don't', he visualizes the cattle-stop and an opening gate.)

'Open the next one.' (There is no pictorial component to the word 'next', so the picture of cattle-stop and opening gate remains foremost in his pictorial brain.)

He drives the quad to the gate by the cattle-stop (it matches the picture still in his head), and he stops and opens it. Job done.

They only stayed half an hour or so, and never really even became a 'client', and I think the farmer would have been more impressed if they could have left with a bottle of pills — each. My answer to the farmer's question of how to *fix* the boy was simply to suggest that he put numbers on the farm gates, and in future refer to those. 'Go up the race, and open gate 8.'

Lizzy

Lizzy was still at school and doing reasonably well, heading for a design and fashion career, but she was thoroughly spooked by her psychic insights and by being targeted by 'dead people'. She reported that these people had always been part of her life as long as she could remember, but the incidence of such events jumped markedly after a minor traffic accident where she took a small bang to the head.

While she previously felt she benefitted significantly from her 'intuitive insights into style and fashion', now, since the accident, her headspace was no longer her own private place, with up to fifteen 'personalities' constantly vying for voice and attention.

In my experience such an extreme situation is not uncommon where a person presents with 'mixed-sidedness', and in Lizzy's case it was a matter of her being right-eyed, left-handed and left-footed. Such a mixture is not rare, but for Lizzy the stress of hormonal maturation, academic pressure, significant end-of-year examinations, together with the shock from the motor vehicle accident, created an overload situation that would probably eventually have led to a 'breakdown'.

She was also (wisely) wary of how any psychologist might respond to her 'weirdness' and was generally fearful of sharing her difficulties with anyone at all. She was well aware that many medical practitioners would see her situation as a 'psychotic episode' and quickly have her on some form of chemical medication.

My overt acceptance of her reality, a little strategic advice on how to manage the 'personalities', and some understanding of the origins of her learning and thinking style allowed her to regain her composure and successfully pursue her creative talent.

Shaun

Shaun's class teacher was the sort of grandmother every child longs for. She was large and warm, both in her physical appearance and in everything she did. She cared deeply about every child she taught, but she was actively worried about Shaun. At seven years, he was the eldest of three brothers, living with their solo father. I could find no reference to or evidence of a mother figure anywhere and the teacher's concerns seemed very well placed.

The given reason for Shaun's referral to my office was that he was stealing lunches, but on enquiry I soon discovered that 'lunches' included anything and everything that any other child brought to school that could possibly fit in Shaun's pants pocket. Although his academic achievement was extremely poor, it was his emotional state that really drew attention. Shaun was emotionally starved.

My visit to the home revealed a house that was physically and emotionally barren. The father's pig-dogs ran amok around and through the house and competed with the three children for food. 'Dad' was thin and wiry, revealed few social skills, but spoke enough to share that he too had been a school failure, that he didn't see a lot of value in 'getting an education' and that, for this family, life was a hand-to-mouth existence. I noted that the backyard of their state rental house was littered with junk including piles of aluminium manhole covers and other metal objects of dubious origin.

I had timed my visit to see Dad in the early afternoon so as to talk without the children present, and to be there when they arrived home from school. I hadn't really taken much notice of the large bowl of white sugar sitting on the kitchen table until Shaun walked in and fed himself several handfuls of the toxic granules.

When I noted to Dad that this granular white poison was not really a healthy option for the lads, and would perhaps be better removed, his very surprised response was, 'But if I don't buy it, what am I going to eat?'

After several weeks working with the family, supplying lunches for the boys and supporting Dad in parenting style, I was stunned to discover that a local health worker had decided to refer Shaun to the local Child Health clinic. There a paediatrician had observed Shaun's erratic energy levels and his lack of focus ability, had quickly labelled him as ADHD — and put him on a regime of Ritalin! No consultation with the health professional who was already working with the family (me), no home-visit to gather background or context, and no interest in getting any understanding of the bigger picture such as family diet, social relationships or emotional needs.

The way in which Shaun presented, the way he acted and was seen to behave, was all just a symptom of his underlying situation, and of his overriding needs. The whole family needed help, not the simple removal of symptoms via chemical medication.

Although I argued my case, the medical team around the paediatrician overruled me, and Shaun's father discontinued our contact. Predictably, Shaun became a Ritalin zombie, presenting no problem at all in the classroom but achieving nothing. Now, 30 years later, he comes regularly to public attention as an illicit trader of other people's property.

So, was Shaun dyslexic? My professional opinion at the time was that Shaun was in such a marginal emotional state that it would have been totally inappropriate to attempt any sort of formal assessment with him. However, his actions were readily observable and he was seen to constantly swap from right hand to left hand, then back again, when involved in any pencil and paper activities. More than this, his speech carried strong dyslexia indicators in that he had a significant lisp, he substituted 'f' for 'th' (e.g. I have free brothers), and his language involved frequent reversals (e.g. fack to bront).

I am committed to the notion that, for the most part, the dyslexic condition is directly linked to left-handedness in the family — and that this is genetic. I frequently work with families where a dyslexic father has low academic ability, suffers consequential low self-concept, and ends up locked into marginal employment and a transient lifestyle. The direct implications for his family are obvious and are usually intensified for any of his children who are overtly dyslexic themselves. These families deserve intensive help, not a quick diagnosis and medication.

Noel

I never actually met Noel, who will always be 21. The coroner's report read 'Death by Misadventure' and proceeded to describe

THE NATURE OF DYSLEXIA

an act of alcohol and drug-fuelled bravado — 'bonnet-surfing' after a party while overseas on a surfing holiday. Standing on the bonnet of a moving car (driven by a mate, but with an interfering jerk in the front-passenger seat), he had been thrown head-first into the kerb and snapped his neck.

Noel was a twin, his brother being a right-hander, and he was a left-hander. The brother was the family star, being seriously academic, and Noel the family clown, skipping school to surf and party.

My conclusion was that like many others I had worked with, Noel was really quite angry and depressed at being 'so dumb', despising himself and living a high-risk lifestyle where if he survived the risky activity he got a personal and social buzz, and if he didn't survive he would be spared any more torture in this life.

I believe few coroners recognize the role of dyslexia in 'Death by Misadventure' cases.

Diane

Diane ('Just call me Di') was twenty and home from uni for the Christmas break. Her campus doctor had recommended counselling for 'nervous tension/emotional breakdown', and she came in with her very concerned mum.

Although Di had met the family requirement by being a model student all through her schooling, achieving easily and well, by the end of her second-year exams — still with good marks — she was a total mess. Not only did she present with very poor coordination — fairly staggering into my office — but she had lost fluency in her speech and sobbed her way through my last box of tissues at a high rate of knots. According to her mother, the only time she regained any semblance of composure was when she played piano (her favourite pastime), playing and faintly singing her own compositions.

I couldn't see any evidence that would point directly to either emotional or physical depression as such, so following an intuitive hunch I asked Di's mother, 'Who is the left-hander in your family?'

With a degree of indignation, she asserted, 'Nobody! There are no left-handers in our family.' We sat in silence for a few seconds, then she added in a more considered tone, 'Well, her grandfather was, but they fixed him!'

Di agreed to do a very quick check of left- or right-sidedness and we discovered that she was left-eyed, left-footed, and although doing all her writing with her right hand, was, at least in my opinion, a very clear left-hander.

I had noticed that Di had used her left hand to stabilize herself as she stumbled into my office, and that nose-wiping was, for her, a distinctly left-handed operation. The (dis)connection between her lack of speech fluency, yet her ease of singing and playing piano, along with the clear demand for high performance from family members, all suggested complications in the arena of lateral dominance — a complication that had been successfully and completely masked by Di's enormous brainpower, and even greater personal drive. The family 'secret' had remained buried and hidden until the academic weight of second-year uni became greater than Di could readily carry.

So what to do? Mum made it very clear that a change to left-handedness was not acceptable to the family at all, so we went with the two-handed piano-playing model — an area of specific comfort and accomplishment for Di.

For the remainder of the long summer break Di worked on her keyboard skills, on her new laptop, with the specific intention of moving away from right-handed writing (taking notes in lectures, and in the creation of her submitted papers). Laptops were few and far between at the time, and Di and her mum made arrangements with uni officials regarding her use of the laptop when sitting exams.

I don't know if left-handedness was ever mentioned in the negotiations, and I can only assume that Di's uni studies continued with the required degree of success.

Emergency first-response crews: Police, Ambulance and Fire

During my many years of practice, I have spent a lot of time working with crew members after traumatic incidents. It very soon became apparent that not only is there a disproportionate number of dyslexic people in these emergency crews, but that they quickly rose through the ranks to become Incident Controllers. That is, until certification and written exams became an issue.

Henry was just one such crew member, but an interesting case in point. As part of a team with a large rural territory encompassing a major arterial highway, Henry was renowned for his uncanny ability to visually absorb enormous amounts of information in just a tiny moment of time — a skill not uncommon in dyslexic people.

His given task was to get to an accident scene as fast as possible, to run his eye over the carnage, then, as other team members arrived, to allocate each a particular aspect and task according to that person's strengths. Many lives were saved as a result of this recognition and application of Henry's natural visual skill — a direct product of the thinking/processing style that creates the language difficulty known as dyslexia.

Henry came specifically to my attention when officialdom demanded that he back up his natural skill with exams and certification. The simple result was that Henry was disqualified by the qualification process. Being dyslexic, he could neither read nor write to pass the exam that would certify him to do the very task that dyslexia made him so good at!

Fortunately, the use of a reader/writer in the exam process, together with an extended time allocation, allowed common sense to prevail.

Top-ranking sportspeople

Similarly, it has been no surprise to me that a significant number of our very top sportspeople — particularly in sports requiring super-fast information assessment, and reactive ability — are overtly (or covertly) dyslexic. Although not all show signs of dyslexia as we would recognize it, their extraordinary visual acuity is a recognizable hallmark.

My clients have included top rally-car racers, motocross racers, ice-hockey goalie, racing-yacht helmsmen — people whose success is directly linked to their ability to perceive, absorb, interpret and respond to a range of complex visual information in a nanosecond. Commonly, when I have acknowledged this and asked how they do it, they have no explanation other than to say that they have learned to value and trust their own body and its innate ability. Perhaps some aspects of dyslexia really can be regarded as a gift (see Chapter Seven).

So the presentations are many and can be radically varied, with the result that the dyslexic person is often seen but not recognized as such. In our next chapter I broaden and deepen our identikit picture by looking beyond the simple 'reading and writing' notion to ask: What else goes with being dyslexic?

Chapter Three
Defining dyslexia

What is dyslexia, really? Here I take a closer look at the child to identify the common pointers which may indicate that they are dyslexic, before including a range of report-card comments that can be equally indicative.

- Defining dyslexia
- Dyslexic ... or not? Do I need to get my child tested?
- Observable characteristics of dyslexia
- Naming and labelling

Defining dyslexia

A Google search throws up the following definition of dyslexia:

'A learning disorder marked by a severe difficulty in recognizing and understanding written language, leading to spelling and writing problems. It is not caused by low intelligence or brain damage.'

This grossly inadequate definition is based on (one section of) the symptoms that an outsider can see — the obvious difficulties in literacy and academic learning — but fails to acknowledge the cause of these difficulties, the fact that dyslexic people think in pictures, not words. And it certainly fails to recognize that the impact of dyslexia goes far beyond the concepts of 'literacy'.

If we presume that dyslexia is simply a literacy issue, we are in danger of sanitizing the issue. In doing so we would stand to cheat the dyslexic person, their family and the teachers, by withholding information. This chapter has been written with the express objective of widening the picture, thus helping the dyslexic person and others associated with them to understand the scope and impact of what they live with on a day-to-day basis.

Without going into any real detail, below is a list of the more common personal characteristics that can go with dyslexia — or, in my terms, with being a pictorial thinker, a 'diesel'. This list has been established from many years of observations while working with dyslexic children and their parents, and as a consultant to industry. There is no attempt to offer any causal explanation for the presence of these characteristics, although a pattern of certain consistencies may become apparent to the reader.

Not all of the characteristics listed here will necessarily be present in any one child, and the apparent absence of any particular characteristic does not diminish the likelihood of them being dyslexic or of having significant learning (and social) difficulties. (Note that this list does not include details of reading/writing difficulties or usual symptoms of a 'learning disorder'.)

As a final note, it is not recommended that this list be used in any way as a *diagnostic tool* or as a means to determine *degree of dyslexia*.

Dyslexic ... or not? Do I need to get my child tested?

Why is it so difficult for teachers, parents and assessors to figure out whether a child fits the syndrome or not?

The main reason is simply that most people have never

been dyslexic themselves so have no personal experience of it, and so do not really know what it is or what they are looking for. Others who have created tests to measure dyslexia might similarly have a distorted view of what it is, and what it is not, and unfortunately the testing process that they generate might reflect this distortion.

The real problem in this difficulty is not that some people might be labelled 'diesel', or dyslexic, when they are not but rather that many people who are dyslexic are not identified as such (or are specifically told they are not dyslexic). They therefore continue to suffer the criticisms, confusions, failure and loneliness without any understanding, empathy or support.

What do we look for in a child or, for that matter, in an adult, that might lead us to check whether this person has a 'different' way of thinking — that perhaps they are dyslexic or are diesel, desperately trying to make sense of a petrol world?

Below are listed characteristics often seen in these people. Caution needs to be exercised here, though. Many 'dyslexics' can read, write and are apparently fluent speakers. Contrary to popular belief, however, this does not stop them from being dyslexic.

In the same way, the fact that a person shows some of the characteristics listed below does not necessarily make them a 'diesel' or dyslexic, and they may not thank you for suggesting so!

However, to facilitate the identification of children in need of support, the characteristics listed may be used by the busy parent or teacher as an initial pointer.

Observable characteristics of dyslexia

Physical

- May be uncoordinated and clumsy, or labelled dyspraxic.
- May not be able to learn 'left' and 'right'.
- May be, or have family members, who are left-handed.
- May walk 'from the hips down'.
- May show *extraordinary* skills in physical coordination and reaction time.
- May have great difficulty in sitting still, or in remaining indoors.
- May persistently be fiddling, touching.

Memory

- May have a very good pictorial memory and what appears to be a poor linguistic (verbal) memory. Pictorial memory is often mistaken for long-term memory.
- May have trouble remembering names or technical terms.
- Often have difficulty with instructions — understanding, remembering and complying with them.
- Instruction that begins with 'Don't' (e.g. Don't spill your drink… Don't forget your…) is likely to create the opposite outcome.

Printing, handwriting and writing

- May use a mixture of uPPeR anD lower-cAse letters.
- May start their printing well out from the margin.
- May prescribe round letters (o, a, b, d, p, q etc.) and numerals in a clockwise, or reverse, direction.

- Letter execution may be very shaky, wobbly or erratic.
- May print some letters backwards — b/d.
- May print whole or parts of words in reverse order.
- May cover up their work from the teacher's view.
- May repeatedly rub out anything that they fear might be less than perfect.
- May repeatedly start new pages after any errors, or even tear pages out of their book.
- May start their writing from the back pages of their book.
- May repeatedly use (known) set phrases.
- May swap the pencil from left to right hands repeatedly.

Reading

- May have a fear and reluctance to read (or even speak) aloud.
- May substitute words.
- May read 26 as 62 (reversal), or as 59 (inversion) or even 95 (reversed inversion).
- May have difficulty with phonics.
- May do reasonably well with assistance but lose all gains very rapidly when it is withdrawn.
- May be unable to enunciate blends.
- May make errors on the small frequently used 'sight words' — is, and, a, the etc.

Speech

- May have very poor enunciation.
- May have a lisp, f/th or w/r substitution, stammer or stutter.

- May resist speaking in public or in front of a critical audience.
- May reverse whole or parts of words.
- May substitute words.
- May use filler words — 'you know', 'like', 'thing', etc.
- May talk non-stop, appear to be eloquent, but have little substance in content.
- May be an erratic speaker, going off on tangents, with constant restarts.
- May be prone to frequent exaggeration and self-promotion.
- May frequently forget what they were about to say.
- May have difficulty finding words to represent their thinking.
- May say things that are highly inappropriate.

Social/behavioural

- May have a very fragile self-concept and low self-confidence levels.
- May enjoy the company of those much younger or much older than themselves.
- May not enjoy team sports.
- May prefer to work/play alone.
- May show nervous reactions, upset tummy etc. in class.
- May set themselves up to be the fall guy or butt of others' humour.
- May work overly hard to get social acceptance.
- May show an overt need to please others.
- May be very sensitive and easily hurt.
- May be highly intuitive.

- May have a wonderful sense of humour and often act the clown.
- May have difficulty with time concepts, telling the time, days of the week.
- May be persistently late or be paranoid about being early.
- May have a fix-it mentality — this may lead them to becoming backyard or professional engineers and tradespeople.
- May show aptitude for technology — the IT world is full of dyslexic problem-solvers.
- May live in a cyber world.
- May be reluctant to move from any task they are currently succeeding on.
- May show an 'addictive' personality.
- May be reluctant to attempt any new task.
- May become fixated with certain skill areas and fanatical about detail in that pursuit.
- May be slow to cooperate or respond to verbal directives.
- May often look confused or 'spaced'.
- May show poor or immature use and understanding of language.
- May often be deep in their imagination and not hear instruction.
- May appear to be deaf.
- May quickly forget verbal instruction.
- May do what they have specifically been told not to do.
- May have a short concentration span — for some activities.
- May be very distractible.
- May have been labelled — ADD, ADHD, ODD, ACC, CPD, APD, GDD, PDD, Asperger's, mildly autistic, manic depressive, schizophrenic.

None of these characteristics alone will indicate dyslexia, but if this list captures the observable style of the child, it is highly likely that this child thinks in *pictures* rather than *words* and has a consequential difficulty in formal learning via the language-based educational system and within the language-dominated classroom setting. This is what dyslexia is about.

Remember, it is not necessarily the case that the 'diesel/dyslexic' can't read; it is more likely to be the case that they *don't* read as they may not even see the print.

Naming and labelling

Unfortunately, 'identification' of any thing or process involves two issues: one is *the process of definition*, and the other is the complicated issue of *naming or labelling it*. While definition is dependent on insight and understanding (a major problem with dyslexia), the labelling debate involves both political and emotional perspectives.

There is huge and ongoing debate as to whether we should label children or not. *Without* a label (e.g. dyslexic), the child may not receive the recognition, special assistance or the tolerance that they really need. On the other hand, *with* a label they may stand to be relegated, sidelined or otherwise written off as a child who is other than 'normal'.

Either way it is human nature to categorize, to group, and to stereotype. Consequently, when we encounter children who do not fit the norm we search for words or phrases to usefully describe them. This is very much the case with children who are often categorized, named and labelled long before they are suspected of having a genuine learning difficulty. Many of these descriptions are naive, blaming and negative, and thus fail to serve the child fairly or well.

Although it may seem to be cynical and unfair, the writer's long experience in primary education has clearly revealed that well before a child is formally diagnosed and categorized as dyslexic (whatever that may mean), they have usually been subjected to repeated negative description and informal labelling that implicitly blames the child and minimizes adult responsibility. These terms, labels or descriptive phrases are generally accusatory and imply fault in the child.

As a rule, if a child's nature or style creates a difficulty or problem for us as adults, we label the child as a 'problem child'. The child gets the blame. Traditionally the teacher-generated 'school report' is where we find such pejorative descriptive phrases, and yet to the insightful observer, they can give an early insight into the needs of the child.

Common descriptors

The descriptors have a certain predictability and may include any of the following:

- 'Does not apply himself consistently.'
- 'Could do better — if she tried.'
- 'Will not settle to the task in hand.'
- 'Intelligent and capable, but with poor attitude.'
- 'Inconsistent attitude — good on his "good" days.'
- 'Ingenious in her strategies of avoidance.'
- 'Attention-seeking — loves to be class-clown.'
- 'Poor concentration and highly distractable.'
- 'Is not satisfied until he has stopped the class and has my undivided attention.'

- 'Is generally away with the fairies — in fantasy land.'
- 'Blames everybody for everything — but never takes responsibility herself.'
- 'Unmotivated and underachieving.'
- 'Will not pay attention long enough to learn.'
- 'If he put as much energy into his own business as he does into everybody else's business, he would fly ahead.'
- 'Poor attitude and commitment to the learning process.'
- 'Generally lazy and unmotivated.'
- 'Has got it — won't apply it.'
- 'Has developed a multitude of avoidance techniques.'
- 'Poor attitude, poor application, poor achievement.'
- 'Generally non-compliant, and disruptive to others.'
- 'Demands a disproportionate amount of teacher time.'
- 'Has an attitude problem.'
- 'The whole class achieves better when she is absent.'
- 'A reluctant learner.'

These descriptors and the characteristics outlined above are a bit like a jigsaw puzzle. Any number of the pieces can be slotted together in an infinite number of ways to create an unpredictable and wildly varying portrait of our dyslexic person. Others may not fit the particular portrait at all.

Chapter Four
Where does dyslexia originate?

> This chapter presents a pictorial model — a visual explanation as to why some children have difficulty with language and present as being dyslexic. I then open a debate as to the wisdom and fairness of such 'medicalized' labels and recommend a substitute: my preferred group descriptor.
> - Where does dyslexia come from?
> - The diesel/petrol analogy
> - So, what is a 'diesel'?
> - What is a self-proclaimed 'diesel thinker'?

Where does dyslexia come from?

The word dyslexia means 'difficulty with language' and refers to what the dyslexic has problems with — the dyslexic is not able to do language very well.

The dyslexic person doesn't do language very well because their brain is wired with a slightly different bias from other people's brains. Just as the female brain has a different style from the male brain, the dyslexic brain is different yet again. The dyslexic brain is not wired in favour of words and language, but rather is wired with specialty skills in visualization and pictorial processing. In short, while most people think mostly with words, the dyslexic thinks mostly with pictures, and has a diminished access to words as a thinking tool. It is common knowledge that some language thinkers have diminished access to pictures as a thinking tool.

The dual brain continuum

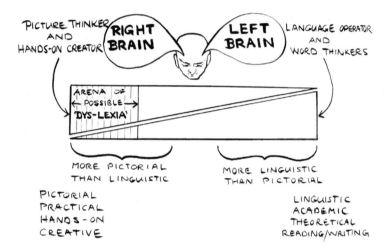

This is not because of low intelligence, and neither is it because of 'brain injury'. It is not 'wrong', and it does not need fixing. The dyslexic way of thinking is a perfectly normal and useful way of thinking — it has its own characteristics, its own strengths and weaknesses. The difficulty arises when we create an educational system that focuses on reading, writing and thinking in words as the preferred style, thus putting the non-word thinker at a considerable disadvantage. This difficulty is then compounded when most of our teachers are 'language thinkers' and are unaware that the perfectly normal-looking child sitting in front of them thinks differently, in a manner they are unaware of, and in a manner that is generally incomprehensible to them.

Although dyslexia has been recognized as a difficulty for a considerable time now, and has been studied by academics in recent years, the value and effectiveness of the research may well have been limited by the fact that it has largely been conducted by academics — who think in words and have never experienced the difficulty of *not* being able to think in words. In effect, they are attempting to study and understand a 'non-language' problem via language.

Historically, dyslexia has been a male domain. Thirty years ago, few girls presented as dyslexic, but some observers now see the rate as rising in girls, as well as in boys. Whether the evidence is now becoming clearer as our understanding grows or the incidence is truly rising remains unclear, but more and more both educational and behavioural difficulties are being seen as the direct result of a degree of dyslexia in the individual concerned.

I have not studied dyslexia as a scientific research topic but have lived with my dyslexia for over 70 years. I have also spent the last 45 years working with dyslexic children, their parents and their teachers. My direct experience and observations from a lifetime of exposure allow me some understanding, insight and clarity, while at the same time acknowledging that there still remains considerable confusion regarding the range of form and degree in which the dyslexic style is presented.

Other dynamics

A range of other dynamics come into play that will determine whether this potential dyslexic child will experience learning difficulties or not — and whether they will *show as dyslexic or not*.

Level of intellect will have a large part to play in the educational success of the child — meaning that the child with less intellectual power will be more susceptible to learning difficulties than the child with greater intellectual resource. By way of analogy, if we consider this child to be like a car towing a trailer — loaded with wet sand — then it becomes very obvious that the size of the engine under the bonnet will have a predictable impact on the way the car performs.

While a smaller, or even medium, allocation of intellectual power may highlight the dyslexic potential of the child, the larger allocation may mask the evidence completely — or it may not.

The amount of exposure to and direct involvement in language in the child's very early years (and sustained through childhood) will also have a significant impact on their learning ability. The child who has extensive exposure to interactional language in their home life (not TV!) will build up a greater vocabulary, giving the advantage of a wider and more extensive verbal toolkit via which to achieve their early educational building blocks. The greater the vocabulary, the more ability to process schooling, the greater the ease of academic achievement. This can mask an otherwise dyslexic style.

The attitude of the home to the child's potential learning difficulties can similarly be a significant factor in their achievement. Predictably, one parent will have had similar experiences at school. If the parents' attitude is *dismissive* of school and of formal education, this will have a negative effect on the child. If their attitude is one of *intolerance* of the child's difficulties, this may have a destructive impact on the child. If the parents are *tolerant and supportive* of the school and of the child, the child's self-concept may be preserved, and the child may not succumb significantly to the difficulties associated with dyslexia — again, potentially masking the impact.

The point of expanding on this array of possible dynamics is to demonstrate why it is so difficult to determine why some children present as dyslexic and others do not. This is also the reason it is so difficult to understand and define what constitutes dyslexia, and why it is so difficult to 'test' for dyslexia in any meaningful way.

The diesel/petrol analogy

A significant undertone to our exploration so far has been a general dissatisfaction with the use of the term, the label, dyslexic. Yes, even with our dislike of the label we have continued to use it, because of the shared recognition it involves.

Now it is time to stand apart, to pick up our own challenge, and to offer a working substitute, an alternative descriptor.

True, there is little chance that the label dyslexic will ever be abandoned by the academics, because it works for them — and they don't have to wear it. But for the child concerned, for their supportive family, and for many teachers, an opportunity to move away from the 'dys' word will be a huge relief.

Let's explore the diesel/petrol analogy, and its prospective benefit.

Dyslexia as a social phenomenon is the product of the absence of language as a useful thinking tool in an individual person. It is most commonly observed in children at the primary level of our education system.

Contrary to popular belief, dyslexia is not a learning difficulty as such. It is more a teaching difficulty, in that it is the style of our 'teaching' system that creates the dyslexic condition.

Consider that our current (western) education system is a recent historical development, evolving through the late nineteenth and twentieth centuries from the egalitarian intention of 'an education for all'. Implicit to this education system, but generally not overtly acknowledged, is the fact that it is orientated to *academia* (rather than overt practicality), and it has a specific reliance on language — as a prime teaching tool, as an information recording and processing tool, and more latterly, as an exclusive assessment tool. So, we see that reading and writing, talking and listening, thinking and problem-solving in words, are the backbone of this education system that we insist every child has to endure. Education has thus become available to all, but there is a catch: in general it has to be accessed via language as a processing tool, a passageway suiting some more than others.

Any child who enters this education system, whose brain functions on a language-based processing style, carries an inherent advantage: lessons are offered according to their own style. Those who have a more practical, hands-on and pictorial-thinking style are actively disadvantaged by this pro-language orientation.

That this situation is simply a historical hiccup is certain, and there is absolutely no suggestion that this is some deliberate political ploy or devious social skulduggery to disadvantage the poor, but in some ways this is exactly what it does.

Dyslexia, therefore, is a punitive social artifact of growing incidence, generated inadvertently by an increasingly language-orientated education system.

So, what is a 'diesel?'

Years of working with children in schools — usually referred for help because of 'learning and behaviour problems' — taught me very quickly that the label dyslexic is not a user-friendly term. Although there will be some children who seem to embrace the label that has been imposed on them, in my experience they are rare.

Watching children who are experiencing both learning and social difficulties noticeably shrink when they hear that they are dyslexic quickly taught me to avoid this term. The spelling of the word, and its technical meaning, are beside the point when these children *hear* the word, and emotionally associate it with all the other negative words that similarly begin with 'dis'.

To be given a label that is so similar to 'disgust', 'disgrace', 'disabled', 'disturbed' and other similar 'dis' words does not sit easily with these children. Their very powerful negative experience indicates that a different word, preferably with positive connotations, is needed.

On discovering that the real essence of dyslexia (and to a large degree Asperger's and autism) is that these children are brain-wired for pictorial and image-based thinking (whereas most people are brain-wired for language-thinking), the parallel with petrol and diesel engines became apparent.

Pictorial-based thinkers tend to decipher language by matching words they hear with pictorial images. They hear 'tennis racket', and they get a distinct related visual image. However, many of our words have no pictorial equivalent. While the word 'ball' has an obvious pictorial association (the image of a ball), and the word 'run' has an immediate pictorial association of an activity, the word 'Wednesday' has no such pictorial equivalent. When a teacher remarks 'In preparation for Wednesday's regular assessment ...' the pictorial thinker has little or no ability to understand the meaning of her words, as none of these (preparation, Wednesday, regular, assessment) has a specific picture. The child may well be able to repeat the words aloud, but they are likely to bear no real significance for them. (I acknowledge that this can be very difficult for a language-thinker to grasp.) Hence, the child is unlikely to prepare for the 'assessment' and will predictably perform poorly.

In such a case, rather than the child having a 'learning problem', we should really say the child has a 'thinking/learning difference'. The teacher is trained in one system (language), but the child operates in another (pictorial images). We could go as far as to say that the thinking-fuel the teacher is offering in good faith in the classroom is not appropriate to the thinking-style of this child. Our teachers are doing what they have been taught to do, and are doing it well, but are unaware of the different style of the child. Frustration, anxiety, anger and depression (for both teacher and child) will predictably follow.

Ron Davis, in his book *The Gift of Dyslexia* (2010), identified approximately 220 words in the English language that do not have a pictorial component. He states that they are the most commonly used words in the English language, making up 75 per cent of our used words. They include: is, and, a, the, too, to, two, was, went, who, what, where, why, how, etc., and at junior levels are referred to as 'sight words' and 'heart words'.

Different fuels

The parallel with petrol and diesel fuels thus becomes apparent. If we put petrol in the tank of our diesel car by mistake, it will not run well — but we don't blame the car for this. If we put petrol (language-based teaching) into the diesel (pictorial) child, they will not be able to perform well — but they tend to get the blame. Unfortunately, because most teachers and parents do not understand this, we inadvertently create an apparent learning difficulty.

Many children of dyslexic style have a strongly practical, hands-on nature, and will be familiar with the ruggedness, strength and usefulness of diesel-powered machinery — bulldozers, tractors, diggers and trucks. They quickly grasp and understand the implications of the 'petrol into the diesel tank' analogy, and many readily embrace the positive associations with 'diesel-power' and take on the appeal of being a 'diesel' learner in a proud and assertive manner.

Although there are a number of characteristics of diesel engines that make this analogy appealing to many, it is not likely that every child will choose to see themselves as a 'diesel', and for their own reasons they may be more comfortable with the traditional labels. But it is important that they have a choice.

So, for those who are attracted to and choose this alternative label, we offer the following explanation.

What is a self-proclaimed 'diesel thinker'?

- A 'diesel', or 'diesel thinker', is a person whose style of thinking would normally lead them to be categorized and labelled as dyslexic.

- Their thinking style is largely characterized by pictorial, or image-based, thinking, as opposed to language-based thinking, and they face a range of difficulties in our language-based society.
- Recognizing their own style and its differences, the 'diesel thinker' chooses not to be assessed, measured, classified and labelled as dyslexic.
- A 'diesel' is a person who chooses to recognize and honour some of their predominating characteristics of personal style — and who at the same time chooses to not impede themselves by accepting a debilitating psycho/medical label.
- Although their thinking style may currently create difficulties for them in the mainstream education system, the 'diesel' chooses to recognize and embrace their style and its differences, proclaiming and claiming their right to be seen as 'normal, but slightly different'.
- They understand that although their style is recognizably different from that of others, rather than there being something 'wrong' with their brain, they have a valid and valued thinking style, highly acute senses, and a practical problem-solving ability that often supersedes that of the 'non-diesel' population of the world.
- A 'diesel' recognizes that if they had accepted the traditional label of dyslexic that this would involve accepting the accompanying notion that they are 'abnormal', that there is something 'wrong' with them, and that they 'don't fit in'.
- The 'diesel' recognizes that if they had accepted that label, and the beliefs that accompany it, they would accept that they are basically in need of therapy, medication or some

similar system of treatment — to 'fix' them, change them, and make them 'fit in'.

- A 'diesel' recognizes and values their own style that makes them a 'diesel', and similarly recognizes the style that characterizes the 'petrols' of the world — and realizes that there is no value for them in ever trying to become one of these.

- A 'diesel' recognizes that this label is positive, descriptive and self-chosen. It is not imposed on them by others, and it does not involve any slur on their style or integrity. Knowing that the 'diesel' style involves a variety of presentations, it leaves them free to claim and demonstrate, in their own way, the degree to which they see themselves as being a 'diesel thinker'.

> **When a driver inadvertently puts petrol into a diesel engine, we don't blame the vehicle for losing power. When a 'pictorial' thinker struggles within a 'linguistic' teaching/education system, typically it is the student who gets the blame.**

Chapter Five
A confusing issue

Having revealed some of the nature of dyslexia, I here offer a few thoughts on why the whole issue remains so confusing and problematic.

- Why is it so hard to get useful information about dyslexia?
- Is dyslexia a product of our education style?

Why is it so hard to get useful information about dyslexia?

Parents and teachers both ask this question with anguish and frustration. They want to help the child, but they are unable to find the practical resources to enable them to do it. Yes, it is hard to get useful information about dyslexia. Although a lot has been written, and more and more 'programmes' are available, there is still a question over the validity of much that has been written.

The answer to the question is semantic, political and academic.

In essence, labelling a person as dyslexic indicates that they don't handle language well. What it doesn't tell us (and only some people yet accept this) is that, as described earlier, the so-called dyslexic person thinks differently from most other people in that, rather than thinking primarily in words, the dyslexic thinks primarily in pictures.

Thinking in pictures as opposed to thinking with words means that the dyslexic is at a disadvantage in a community that uses verbal language as a prime communication tool. In western society it is standard to think in language, to communicate by speaking language, to participate by listening to language, to write and read language, and to govern and teach using language. Few of us would ever stop to consider this, and most of us happily participate in our language environment without any thought to examine the plight of the person whose thinking style does not involve language.

So part of the answer to this question (Why is it so hard…) would lie in the basic lack of a full and useful understanding of just what dyslexia really involves — and that makes sense. The hard part is accumulating sufficient knowledge to move on from there.

A typical dyslexic?

Unfortunately, there is no such person as a 'typical dyslexic', and this is part of the confusion. Such an imprecise label can at best have only an umbrella function, allowing for the loose collection of a confusing variety of presentations, which themselves are the product of interactions of a range of dynamics. These presentations vary considerably for known and unknown reasons, and include factors such as gender, 'intelligence', and familial history of left-handedness. But they also include a range of extraneous dynamics such as the individual's history of support, neglect or outright abuse by authority adults in their life — such as parents and school teachers — and even such banal dynamics as the suburb of the town they live in.

Predictably, a personal history involving positive encouragement from family and teachers (as opposed to pressure), full exposure to language in the family of origin, and previous support with positive and useful teaching strategies will also make a significant (and positive) impact on the way a dyslexic child will present.

As stated above, a further major dynamic determining the apparent degree of dyslexia will be a person's level of resource in terms of sheer brainpower that they can draw on when coping with the challenges their disability creates. It is self-evident that the more processing equipment a child has the better they may handle their degree of language deficit.

These variables within the individual child will in some cases even operate so as to mask the fact that they are dyslexic in the first place — further fuelling the debate as to what a 'real dyslexic' would look like and confusing the availability of useful information to parents and teachers alike.

Politics

As is frequently the case, politics has an insidious impact here as well. The predominant political and educational philosophies at the time may determine the degree of support available for a child.

Universities

This observation begs the question of university-based, academic research, its relevance and potential contribution to the pool of useful information about dyslexia.

In the experience of the author, one of the biggest impediments to academic research on dyslexia lies in an implicit conflict between the very nature of dyslexia itself and the linguistic basis of academic research. As we acknowledged earlier, by definition the term dyslexia indicates that the person has significant difficulty with language. Acknowledging that language lies at the very essence of academic achievement and success, it is self-evident that the child with dyslexia — especially a serious case — is unlikely to experience academic success and is consequently unlikely to pursue educational studies beyond the minimum that the law requires. In simple terms, they leave school as soon as they can.

This indicates that few 'dyslexics' are likely to make 'the science of education and learning' a topic of further academic study on leaving school. From this it is obvious that those who study dyslexia, who research and write about it, are most likely, by definition, not dyslexic. They are language-proficient, they are academic, and this style will characterize their perspective. Although they may study, make deductions and learn, they will never *know* dyslexia, because knowledge can only come from direct personal experience.

Research

In research, despite the rigorousness of the scientific method, the scope of the external observer is always constrained by the need to interpret and draw conclusions from what they observe. Although a researcher might have evidence in front of them, they might not recognize it as such, and as a consequence, certain information may not ever be considered or taken into account. On the other hand, evidence may be seen and recognized, but often misunderstood, misconstrued or misread, allowing partial or even false conclusions to be drawn.

More than this, however, academic research is typically dependent on questions or proposals and certainly on language-based thinking. In this the researcher must ask questions or set up proposals to be checked, proved or disproved. This process depends on the initial validity of the researcher's observations, and on their information-gathering procedures — sometimes even depending directly on questions that the researcher asks participants, in this case 'dyslexics'.

We know that 'dyslexics' don't understand language very well, and those of us experientially familiar with the area also recognize that this means that the dyslexic person's understanding of a question may be quite different from that of the researcher. Further, their response — especially if it is in words — may not accurately represent what they mean. (Remember; the dyslexic frequently has trouble finding then selecting words that relate usefully to the pictures or feelings in their head. When they do find words, they are likely to be only a first approximation, rather than an accurate description of what the person means. And then the dyslexic runs into their next problem, their mouth — the words that the tongue and mouth next utter may not be the ones that they meant to say as an answer at all.)

Like many other teachers and parents, I have long been frustrated by the lack of useful information on dyslexia as a learning difficulty, and I have even more so been frustrated by some of the claims made by educational professionals and academics around the issue. Seldom does their information and claims match my lifelong experience of dyslexia.

Recently an 'international expert' (a professor from the UK) admitted under questioning that his 'world-leading research into dyslexia' was done using a group of university students as his dyslexic sample! Is it not totally obvious that such a privileged group of high-ability people are not at all representative of the population he is purporting to investigate? What social or academic bias lies behind such a basic error?

My specific objective so far has been to highlight the centrality of the pictorial thinking style as being problematic in a language-based education system. Identifying such a thinking style as being common, different, but 'normal' shifts the perceived problem-base from the child to the system. There is nothing wrong with the dyslexic brain — it just needs to be recognized, accepted and catered for within our overriding pedagogy.

Is dyslexia a product of our educational style?

Dyslexia is most commonly associated with children in an educational setting — why?

The answer to this question lies in this potentially inflammatory statement: *If we didn't have a formal education system, it is almost certain that we would not have any social difficulty called dyslexia. Dyslexia as we know it is a direct product of the nature of our approach to education.*

Our education system is a language-dominated beast — and few of us would consider that it could be otherwise. Indeed, language (be it spoken or written) is our prime chosen means of communication, and our predominant system for imparting information and knowledge. We use language to process information — to hold it, to describe it, to record it, to share it, to extend it, to explore it, to develop it, to teach it — and then to measure the effectiveness of our teaching.

Because our educational processes are language dependent, it stands to reason that our assessment of educational issues such as 'teaching effectiveness' and 'learning effectiveness' are also language dependent. We engage children with the implicit assumption (a 'teaching truth') that language and its use as a thinking and processing tool is a commonality. For the most part we are safe in this, and the clear evidence is that it works well for the majority of our population. However, when we unwittingly deal with a 'pictorial thinker' in this way, we (and that individual) can very quickly come unstuck.

The 'pictorial thinker' typically does not recognize themselves as such, as few of us ever stop to ask ourselves, 'How do I think?' In a classroom there is little about the external physical appearance of this child to indicate to any teacher their point of difference. Thus, for years our educationalists have assumed that language is the basic and natural system of thinking for all learners. Unfortunately, this assumption has led them to draw negative conclusions about the intellectual capacity of children whose thinking style has been other than linguistic. In the extreme they have even been seen to be 'slow learners' or 'learning disabled'.

The very label we have given them clearly demonstrates that we view them as being in deficit — dyslexic means 'difficulty with language' — and they have traditionally been sidelined on this basis. (Although educationalists may protest this point, the lifelong experience of adult 'dyslexics' is consistent.)

So what to do? What can we do here that we can be sure is more useful than what has been offered in the past?

It becomes tempting to ask: 'What means can we devise to usefully and fairly assess children's intelligence and learning abilities, allowing for the discrepancy between our language-dependent style and their non-language style?'

As appropriate as this challenge might initially seem to be, perhaps it is even more pertinent to ask: 'Is it morally and ethically defensible to attempt to measure a concept so personal, so extensive, and so indefinable as "intelligence and learning ability"?'

In risking opening a huge can of worms, I can only say that I have not yet encountered or devised a test, a technique or a strategy that I am convinced will ethically, fairly and validly achieve such an educational yardstick.

But moving beyond this ethical and philosophical dilemma, back to the point of this page, how do we identify a dyslexic child in the classroom? Beyond this, once we have potentially identified the child, we are then faced with yet another ethical question: 'Is it really necessary, or even appropriate, to have this identification formally confirmed, and the child tagged with such a permanent, negative socio-educational label?'

In the following chapters, I expand exploration into the personal and social implications of the dyslexic thinking style as a daily-life issue. The objective is to extend the information as we know it, to add it to the pool, so that parents, teachers and children may all benefit and develop expertise for use in the future.

> **Dyslexia in the classroom does not so much demonstrate a learning difficulty, but rather a pedagogy and teaching issue.**

Chapter Six
Labels, definitions and myths

Here we enter a brief discussion about the processes and the ethics of labelling and defining issues that we really don't understand well. We then proceed to present some of the common misunderstandings (myths) around dyslexia and, focusing on ADHD, we demonstrate the danger of labelling, defining and responding to our partial understandings and misunderstandings.

- Labels
- Definitions
- Common myths about dyslexia
- ADD and ADHD

Labels

Medicine, psychology and psychiatry are awash with labels, often of Greek or Latin origin, which do not in themselves have any clear or obvious meaning to members of the general public. Specialists within these areas of study use labels as a mechanism to categorize illnesses or behaviours, or the persons they identify as showing symptoms of these 'illnesses' or behaviours.

Labels are seldom positive in their messaging, and the person so labelled has little say or choice in the matter. The process can be socially savage. Typically labels with a negative social loading are selected and ascribed by others, who by dint of their training and qualifications are assumed to have skills and knowledge that are up to the task. Society grants them the power and high social status for doing so. But to what advantage for whom?

Our socio-medical system leans towards identifying and labelling persons who do not quite fit the social norm. Although this is not at all new, there is some concern that in recent years this has started to get out of hand, with the number of registered 'conditions' and labels multiplying dramatically (such as in the *Diagnostic and Statistical Manual of Mental Disorders, 4th Edition* — DMS-IV) and ignoring the sidelining implications that typically further sabotage the life-chances of the person left carrying that label. The labels are applied under the guise of providing 'support', and of ensuring 'protection', for both the individual and the general public — should they need it. But what benefit does a label such as dyslexic bring to an individual child, or adult, and how readily can that person escape the social prejudices that might be associated with the label?

A quick look at the very term dyslexia reveals that it is a negative statement — it translates (from Latin) as 'difficulty with language'. At best it tells us what the child has difficulty with, what they are not able to do, and leaves us completely in the dark as to what the child does do or has skills in.

The term dyslexia constitutes a specifically negative label (the 'dis' sound has few positive relatives in the English language), conveying no useful or constructive information and would, I argue, be best abandoned, and replaced by a more socially appropriate descriptor, as suggested in Chapter Four.

The 'lexia' part of the label refers to lexicon, from the Latin and Greek meaning 'language' or 'of or for words'. Yes, dyslexia is all about language, and the fact that dyslexic people — a significant section of our community — struggle to use language as a useful thinking and learning tool. The real significance of this lies in the fact that school is a language-based institution.

Social developments over the last 200 years have brought a change in style, a change in values — and a change in education. 'Educational opportunity for all' may be a fair and valid ideal, but in practice this notion may well have blinded us to the realities of individual learning style — and our ideal may be the very factor that has created the dyslexic phenomenon. The positive value of universal educational opportunity may have been negated for many children by the presumption that *language is the preferred or even the prime mode of learning.*

To this observer it is no coincidence that dyslexia as a learning difficulty has appeared and evolved at the very same time that our educational approach, our style of presentation and evaluation, and our notion of educational 'success' have become aligned with notions of 'literacy' as such.

Picture Thinker   **Language Thinker**

In crude brevity, the usefulness of the label dyslexia is likely to be eroded by a number of factors:

- Under the age of twelve years most boys tend to be 'pictorial' thinkers anyway.
- In some cases, the sheer intellectual capacity of the individual may mask (or not) the child's processing style and any associated learning difficulty.
- The degree of early exposure to language in the child's home will affect the development of their language toolkit — or not. (TV will not usefully extend the individual's vocabulary.)
- Commonly used psychological assessment tools may give a misleading read-out of what the child's real abilities (and therefore real difficulties) are.
- If a child struggling in the classroom setting learns that they are dyslexic, they are likely to associate this label with all the other 'dis' words they know, with predictable emotional consequences.

Definitions

In order to examine and educate ourselves about dyslexia we need an insightful definition, and a means of identifying characteristics that indicate the dyslexic style. Here we meet 'horse and cart', 'chicken and egg' complications.

A definition presumes a full and adequate understanding of the topic in hand — as a definition based on partial knowledge stands to be misleading and dangerous. It could be inadequate, it could be sweeping and overly inclusive, and it may involve inappropriate assumptions. As mentioned elsewhere in this book, this has long been a difficulty in the study of dyslexia, as most of the 'experts' discussing the topic are disadvantaged by being able to study it only from the outside observer's point of view.

Unfortunately, most definitions available reflect the limited perspective of the outside observer — a totally understandable limitation in that most researchers, writers and commentators are by definition academics and therefore linguistic thinkers. It is most unlikely that they have ever experienced dyslexia as a personal domain. These people describe dyslexia as they observe it, as it appears to them, and by its most obvious and consistent presentation. Hence, dyslexia is most frequently identified, defined and limited as a *reading and writing difficulty* — because, to them, this is what it looks like.

Thus, confusion prevails as to what dyslexia may or may not involve, and a proliferation of attempts at creating a definition have further confused the professional bodies responsible for the hands-on education of our young. Those involved at a personal level — the children, their parents and their teachers — deserve the support of an adequate and useful definition to use as a guide, in order to be able to identify which children to address in which particular way, so that their educational and personal needs might be best met and their life-chances preserved.

My own experience as a dyslexic child, then adult, and my professional interaction with struggling 'dyslexics', clearly indicates that many descriptions and definitional attempts focus on 'tip-of-the-iceberg' characteristics. In doing so they detract from the real enormity of the syndrome, failing to recognize the 'ship-sinking' and life-threatening potential of what lies under the surface. In not recognizing the wider dynamics, such definitions risk effectively denying their existence, and unwittingly collude in blaming and abandoning the dyslexic to their fate.

It is perhaps a little ironic that national welfare systems readily pump enormous amounts of money into dealing with the downstream lifestyle and social repercussions of what we call dyslexia (drugs and alcohol, unemployment, crime), but have been traditionally shy of any serious attempts at a constructive preventative approach to what can constitute a lifelong ailment — or, in better circumstances, a life-enhancing strength.

Continuum of style

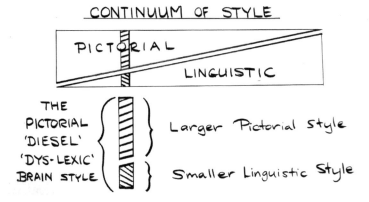

The dual-brain continuum presented in Chapter Four gives rise to the continuum of style (above), which in many ways provides the best graphical understanding of the basis of the functioning of the dyslexic brain. The reader will quickly see the probable impact of differing positions to the right or left in this simplified pictorial explanation.

Sometimes the endeavour to establish an understanding of what something *is* can be most readily assisted by initially establishing what it *is not*.

On this basis we will therefore now pay a little attention to looking at what dyslexia *is not* ...

Common myths about dyslexia

Many commonly held beliefs as described below (which we often don't even realize we hold!) allow us to keep blaming the child for their own difficulties. This is yet another social arena where the victim gets the blame.

MYTH: 'They grow out of it by the time they turn twelve'/'It is just a childhood thing'/'They grow out of it at puberty'

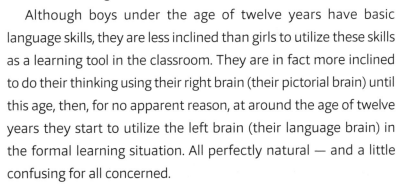

This is based on the observation that it is relatively common for male students to struggle with linguistic learning until around the age of twelve years, but somehow they seem to 'come right' after this.

Although boys under the age of twelve years have basic language skills, they are less inclined than girls to utilize these skills as a learning tool in the classroom. They are in fact more inclined to do their thinking using their right brain (their pictorial brain) until this age, then, for no apparent reason, at around the age of twelve years they start to utilize the left brain (their language brain) in the formal learning situation. All perfectly natural — and a little confusing for all concerned.

Girls (in the same age group) are brain-wired somewhat differently and show a greater inclination to utilize the skills of their left (language) brain — for socializing, communicating — and for learning. Their achievement levels in this seem to be somewhat enhanced by the fact that their left brain apparently has up to *eight* specific sites independently dedicated to various functions of language. Their male counterparts have only *one* (Pease 2001).

Dyslexia usually becomes apparent in the early years (seven to nine years) because the child's left-brain, language facility is not their area of strength, and their natural right-brain, pictorial style does not fit well with our formal language-based teaching approach.

In some cases, the picture becomes confused when dyslexic children of higher intellectual capacity learn to strategize and cover as they grow older, or alternatively work extraordinarily hard in order to scrape by and achieve an average pass. In this way they can mask their dyslexia, leading observers to believe that they have actually grown out of it.

The really sad thing about this myth is that it implicitly blames the child for the difficulties they experience, in that it fails to recognize what is really going on for them.

MYTH: 'It is a minor brain dysfunction, and they need rewiring or recalibrating'

Just as the outside form of the human body can present with many variations (tall, short, stocky, slender, etc.), the inside wiring and, more importantly, the natural style of the inside wiring, differs from one person to another.

The two sides of our frontal brain (the home of conscious thinking) are quite different, and as mentioned above, gender has a further impact on this altogether. In very general terms the left brain is the home of language and linguistic thinking, and the right brain is the home of the pictorial thinking style. Typically, women have more orientation to the left, language facility, and men more to the right, pictorial style.

Neither side is right or wrong, nor is either side in itself preferable or more valuable than the other. The difficulty comes when we teach according to one style (the language style), rather than the other, or both. (As outlined earlier, I find it useful to suggest that 'language thinkers' are like petrol-engined cars, and that 'pictorial thinkers' are like diesel-engined cars, and that school is like a petrol station where the diesel cars are filled up with petrol. These children do not need changing — they just need to be taught appropriately).

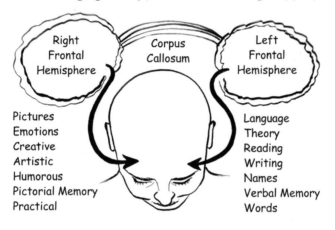

Right Frontal Hemisphere

Corpus Callosum

Left Frontal Hemisphere

Pictures
Emotions
Creative
Artistic
Humorous
Pictorial Memory
Practical

Language
Theory
Reading
Writing
Names
Verbal Memory
Words

MYTH: 'Dyslexia is where kids read "was" for "saw" and write their letters backwards — it's a reading and writing thing'

Although parents and teachers see reversals and associated reading/ writing difficulties in the dyslexic child, few people recognize the origins of the reversals (the implicit right to left process orientation), or the constant mental and emotional exhaustion produced by having to learn the basic educational skills in what is for them a 'back to front' direction. This entire book is my attempt to deal with this myth.

Few people have a useful understanding of dyslexia — not even the 'dyslexics' themselves, even though they live with its impact every day of their lives. The real implications are huge, account for a major part of our national social-welfare costs and extend to include a disproportionate number of our single-parent families and of our prison population.

MYTH: 'It is just in boys'

At one stage it did seem that dyslexia was a male thing, but over recent years the incidence in girls has risen markedly. It is thought that girls are better at hiding or masking their dyslexia and it is often not uncovered until later in secondary schooling or university years.

In a nutshell, the more language-based our assessment system becomes, the greater the proportion of picture-thinkers will fail those assessments. To be blunt, I suggest that by 'refining' assessment systems and making them more language-based, we are creating more and more educational 'failures'.

It makes no sense at all to me that in order to qualify as a builder or a plumber (hands-on, visual, practical pursuits) a person must pass exams about plumbing based on reading and writing skills. Recently, written exams have been introduced for a formal qualification in sheep shearing!

The evolution of the human male over the history of the species, as the hunter and the defender (as opposed to the female role, predictably more aligned with nurturing and social communication/ relationships) could well explain the practical, hands-on and *pictorial style* that we regard as stereotypically male. The later evolution of our formal education system, with its progressively increasing orientation to and reliance on *linguistic processing*, could well account for the difficulties our boys experience in school, for their disengagement, and our current problem with truancy.

MYTH: 'Medication is needed'

There are some people who think this way, who see unwanted behaviour as being a product of an 'imbalance of chemicals in the brain' and see medication as the way to fix such ailments. All I can say to this is 'Sorry, *no*.'

MYTH: 'It can be fixed' — by programmes, by repetition, by practice

Actually, as the reader will understand by now, it is not broken, so does not need to be fixed. But what we do need to fix is our poor understanding of how the child thinks, and then modify our way of teaching and assessing, and of communicating with the child.

MYTH: 'Dyslexic kids are really just lazy or dumb and stupid'

As strange as it may seem, of all the myths, this is the one I could most readily excuse. Often, for teachers and parents who are doing the very best they know how, this is how it seems. In their frustration they often tell me: 'I know he hears what I say, he is not deaf, and he can repeat it back to me, and he is certainly not dumb — so it must be deliberate disobedience.' Such a statement is fully correct, until we make that last assumption — which is really just an expression of our own frustration.

This is an unfortunately common statement, and it is the indicator of a teacher or parent who has given up on a child, who has lost all patience and tolerance. This situation comes about when a teacher has tried *everything*, or at least everything that they know, and nothing has worked. In this, such a response is understandable but not acceptable.

But *understanding* is the key issue. Few classroom teachers really have a good understanding of what is going on for the child, and so, despite their efforts, they are not able to deal with it in a useful way. Hopefully, with the support of this book, teachers will be able to view these children differently, work with them differently, and together achieve a more positive outcome.

MYTH: 'All dyslexics are potential artists'

It may or may not be the case that absolutely all 'dyslexics' think in pictures — I am very happy to allow exceptions to any rule — but I don't recall ever working with any dyslexic person who did not have a significant orientation to their pictorial, creative, artistic, hands-on, musical, intuitive or emotive side. However, such an orientation does not in any way equate with merit or skills as an artist. Yes, we can say that many creative people are dyslexic, but any more than this becomes a myth.

MYTH: 'If they can read or write they can't be dyslexic'

This is confusing because many dyslexic people can either read or write (often one, but not the other), and some can even do both — and still be dyslexic. However, if a parent or teacher buys into the belief that dyslexia is simply a reading and writing difficulty, it is understandable that they might accept this myth. Hopefully, by the time the reader has reached this point in the book, they will have a much deeper appreciation of what the dyslexic is living with and realize that the label itself is unfortunately misleading.

Two other points are worth noting here. The first is that although the person may be able to 'read' the words aloud, this does not mean that they are able to understand the message that they bear — they may not be able to extract the meaning. They might even understand each separate word but still not be able to decipher what they mean as a sentence. We could describe this person as 'barking at print', but not really reading.

The second point is that, yes, a person might really be able to read, but how hard is it for them to do this, how accurately are they reading, and to what level of difficulty can they read? Most popular magazines are written at around a twelve-year reading level and many are aimed at a level below even this.

So, yes, your rather intelligent, 35-year-old adult might be able to read a popular international magazine such as *Reader's Digest* and still be dyslexic

MYTH: 'If they can read, they should be able to write; if they can write, they should be able to read'

Unfortunately, many teachers and parents buy into this one, effectively blaming the child for the difficulty they are having. Although we commonly lump reading and writing together as if they are two sides of the same coin, they are far from

this, and neurologically they utilize quite different processes of the brain. Some people rationalize that the material a child reads is the same as the output of their writing (words), and although an adequate explanation of this is far too complex for this current edition, this must be dismissed as yet another myth.

MYTH: 'They are not dyslexic, they are just dyspraxic (or have dyscalculia)'

Having worked with many thousands of children with learning difficulties, my observation is that the coordination difficulties we associate with dyspraxia (untidy or messy handwriting) are the product of the same left/right sidedness complications that lie behind dyslexia. Indeed, the so-called 'not dyslexic dyspraxics' are simply those people with fine motor coordination issues, who one way or another disguise their associated dyslexic difficulties.

Children who present as having difficulty with number concepts (but are otherwise achieving satisfactorily in school) are often referred to as having dyscalculia. In my experience these people are pictorial thinkers who for one reason or another are attempting to process number as a *linguistic* concept. They would be better to learn to process number as a *pictorial* concept.

MYTH: 'They are an intelligent person — they are not dyslexic!'

The fact that the car has a V8 engine under the bonnet does not stop it from being a diesel. Dyslexia is associated with a pictorial thinking style and an associated difficulty in processing thought via language. Actual intelligence is another thing altogether.

What is really happening here is that the person in question has probably devised all sorts of clever strategies to overcome and to mask or hide their difficulties. On the surface they seem to be performing well, but under the surface, like the proverbial duck, they are working so hard! This person, be they child or adult, really would benefit from having a clear understanding of their own style, their own strategies, and their own difficulties.

MYTH: 'They can read when they want to — no way are they dyslexic, just lazy'

Rather than showing that the child is not dyslexic, this statement amply demonstrates the power of motivation. It is hard to believe that some teachers would think that a child would *choose* to be a non-reader if the skill was readily within their grasp.

Speaking as author of this book, although to an extent I can write, I find reading very hard work, and an unpleasant task. I would prefer to mow the lawn or dig the garden. Not only are they more enjoyable for me, but easier to do and far more satisfying for my brain style. Good readers find this difficult to believe, mainly because they can't understand that an intelligent, educated person could possibly find reading that difficult. But it is, I assure you, and not through lack of trying.

However, when I am faced with text on a topic of high personal interest, I bite the bullet and persevere — for a time, until I get what I want, get to the end or simply get exhausted.

Discovering a child's topic of fascination and interest may well lead the teacher to a child's point of motivation. Work with this, gently and sensitively, and they may well learn to read. But remember, they may never do this for recreational purposes — they may never become 'a reader'.

Additional comments

- Particular passing circumstances (e.g. trauma, or emotional or physical stress) can create a 'temporary dyslexic state' in otherwise 'normal' people. This can occur in both men and women who are normally eloquent and linguistically articulate but who under specific stress lose their skill, becoming temporarily dazed and incompetent, and afterwards regretting what they *didn't* say. Imagine living your life like this all the time. That is what many 'dyslexics' have to live with.

- Many apparently 'normal' people are actually quite dyslexic but go to great lengths to hide it and disguise their difficulties, fearing that it actually demonstrates an inadequacy, a weakness or deficiency. This fear often lies behind their tendency to perfectionism.

- For many, their *pictorial thinking style* is their superior strength in life, and the source of their particular genius. Dyslexia may not be a 'gift', but it's not all bad.

- For others who have suffered the difficulties, the failures and the put-downs during their schooling, the humiliation involved actually creates an almost obsessive reactive determination to achieve and 'succeed' — whatever that means to them — and these people sometimes become our highest fliers, in a variety of ways.

So there go the myths. But why were they ever there in the first place?

Before we leave this area of examination, we need to make a thorough exploration of the whole area known as ADD/ADHD: what it is, and more specifically what it is not.

ADD and ADHD

Attention deficit disorder (ADD) and attention-deficit/hyperactivity disorder (ADHD) — although these labels are not really of *myth* status, they should only be used with warning signs, police cordons and paramedics at the ready. Together they constitute a horrifically dangerous piece of terminology that has been ascribed the status of 'diagnostic label' and used frequently as an offensive blunt weapon upon already-damaged children.

Therefore, proceed with caution.

A very telling insight can be gained by examining how any particular society (animal or human) deals with aberrant behaviour — or at least those members of society whose behaviour differs significantly from that of those who hold the power. One of the most common systems used in human society is 'name calling', and in very recent times western societies have adopted (and whitewashed) this strategy under the banner 'Name it and shame it'. This is indeed a very powerful combination of bullying and labelling.

As useful, powerful and effective as this is in the right circumstances, it can be equally damaging when used without wisdom and understanding.

What do you mean, ADD, ADHD?

It seems to go with being a boy — being accused of being ADD or even of being ADHD. Yes, 'accused' — as these labels are seldom used in a sympathetic tone, and more often reflect an element of frustration, exhaustion and intolerance in a teacher or parent faced with 'normal' boy behaviour.

In terms of style, boys seem to have a need to be overt, noisy, physical and loud — as if hearing the echoes resounding off their environment confirms their very existence. It has even been suggested that this is how males determine and confirm their presence, their identity: the noisier they are the more real they are. Or is it perhaps the other way around: that the more insecure they are, the more need they have to express their presence through such overt means as noise, or at least loud visual image.

Boys stomp and crash, whereas girls giggle and talk. Girls preen themselves in the mirror — for hours on end — while boys roar through the town (peripheral vision glimpsing flashes of reflection in plate-glass frontage) on their Harleys. Women 'multitask', using their exclusive endowment of eight separate cranial language sites, like a linguistic octopus, to the confusion and often-times chagrin of their linguistically short-changed male counterparts. And our sons get labelled ADD or hyperactive.

'Attention deficit disorder' (ADD) is a moniker often bandied around with very little close examination or understanding of what is really going on, but that is par for the course in the whole arena of dyslexia. The words themselves would suggest that the culprit has some lack of ability, or even some lack of willingness, to engage with learning activities at an intellectual level. The label is commonly accompanied by the descriptor 'highly distractible', but with a slight tonal hint of accusation, suggesting an element of anger or intolerance by the speaker, invariably the parent or class teacher of the accused.

'Attention-deficit/hyperactivity disorder' or ADHD becomes a double-barrelled tag, additionally endowing the individual with a physical style that might match that of a cornered wild cat — leaping from door handle to curtain rail in perpetual frenzy, or at least at levels that prevent any associate or family member having any predictable peace.

Such labels, it would seem, are not self-descriptions. They are invariably invented and imposed by other people, by outsiders, who have themselves never participated in or been subject to the particular affliction at a personal level. These people label what they *see*, as opposed to what they *know*.

But, as with the rest of dyslexia, from the inside the story is different, and needs to be explored and exposed.

The senses

How many senses do we have? Our various senses all operate individually and so at any one moment we may be subject to signals through our eyes, our ears, our skin, our nose and our tongue — all signals being received simultaneously. Our eyes, ears and skin may in fact each be bombarded by literally thousands of signals at any one moment. Could we ever begin to measure how many visual signals our eyes are subject to every instant? And the same goes for the ears and the skin — all this meaning that the human sensory system is receiving saturation input much of the time.

Fortunately, to protect us from burnout, a compensatory protective shield is deployed where our major internal computer scans, sorts and prioritizes the items in this sensory flood, ascribing preference and priority to a very small proportion of the available input. This allows us to select and focus, to effectively pay attention to what we regard as most important at that moment. Thank God for such an effective neurological system — what would life be like without that screening ability!

Good question. And if you want a good answer, just ask the ADD child, because this is what daily life is like for them.

For reasons beyond our current knowledge, the children we

label as ADD have a significant deficit in terms of this protective screening device, and their 'attentional energies' are perpetually hammered by an enormous array of input that they are unable to block, sort or selectively prioritize. Every sound, whether natural or artificial, demands identification and attention, while at that same moment every movement within their direct or peripheral vision vies for visual contact. Just watch their eyes and get a glimpse of what they are taking in.

Every exhausted adult knows what it is like to be bombarded by other people's noise — stereos, lawnmowers, radios, TV, children crying — all at the same time, and we need it all to just *shut up!* We also need to understand that this is the everyday reality of the 'ADHD' child.

But there is more.

Equally, every available smell, natural, industrial or human, will be beelining the nostrils of this child, stacking up for olfactory analysis — as will the tactile interference of air movement past the hairs of their leg, the rumble through their chair of the truck someplace beyond the wall, and that elusive itch somewhere on their scalp or in the seat of their pants. Addressing those that they can, trying to ignore those that they can't, and fighting off the intrusions of the many more that overload their sensory system becomes a seriously exhausting continuous routine for the ADD/ADHD child.

Question: So does the child really have an ADD problem? Answer: No, not at all. There is no attention *deficit* here. What you are observing is rather a very clear and equally extreme *attention overload* situation that dominates their very existence.

In many ways we would be better to label this child as experiencing AOD (attention overload difficulty), and ironically this different understanding immediately puts question to the real value of the intentionally stimulating environment our teachers often promote and value in our classrooms.

Impact on the child

As the reader would expect by now, there is more to this situation than meets the eye.

The child with AOD experiences three real sets of difficulty: the first and most obvious is a consequential difficulty in applying themselves to their set task, with a downstream impact on educational learning being quite predictable. The other two are more insidious, and in themselves are perhaps even more personally crippling.

Let's look at the first difficulty: applying themselves in the typical classroom environment. There, they are accompanied by 25 other children graciously providing a cacophony of noise — talking, laughing, scraping chairs, dropping pencils — in a room that frequently is constructed to magnify all sound. Colourful artwork is displayed on all available walls and strung on wires to move in any possible breeze so as to stimulate the peripheral vision. And then there are all the odours that 25 children can generate and share ... Most of the children will cope with this, but for our child who so often gets blamed for disrupting the class, this is torture, perpetuated torture.

The second is the attitude of the adults in the child's life. The parents and teachers of this individual might not realize that they are subject to an overload of sensory input that they cannot cope with or control, and of which they have no knowledge. With good intention they cajole them for not paying attention, for not concentrating (their energies) on the task in hand, for being distractible and for 'drifting off into fantasy'. So often they are publicly admonished and penalized for something they are completely unable to control. They are drowning in the pulses of life.

The third is that the child has no notion that they are different in this regard, and that the bombardment they experience is not the norm. They experience life as they know it, and like everybody else, they assume that this is normal. It does not appear to them to be an abnormal bombardment — it is just as it has always been — it just is. They know that other children don't react as they do, and the child doesn't understand this difference, so they accept the blame.

The upshot of these three difficulties is that as well as having a consequential learning difficulty, the child is blamed for being uncooperative by the people important to them, and the child, in their naivety, accepts the label, the blame and the responsibility. Anxiety, anger, a low self-concept and eventually depression are the predictable outcomes.

ADHD — a personal comment

If this label had been around when I was a child (some 60 years ago), I would have been forced to wear it! Here it deserves a quick examination, an exploration that might throw more light on what is a dark episode of my own life.

In the very early 1950s the world (and yours truly) was introduced to the wonders of 'cordial', a thirst-quenching, flavoured and virtually addictive drink, aimed directly at the child market. A particular version was sold under the cute name 'Jungle Juice'. This mix-and-serve concoction came in small sachets, ready to combine with four pints of water and six cupfuls of sugar. Its presence heralded the beginning of an international marketing programme designed to enrich the investors despite the overt damage to the clientele. The programme continues today albeit with a wider variety of canned 'soft' drinks.

As a 'go-faster' recipe, it was a full competitor to aviation fuel and sent my fly-weight system into a self-destructive spin that the family doctor could neither understand nor explain, as at that time in history personal diet was not a topic of discussion.

The muscles in my legs and arms pulsed with electrochemical energy, creating fast and erratic movement, and I could neither sit nor concentrate for more than a few seconds at a time. Teachers, family, siblings and friends soon ran out of tolerance, and I quickly became a lonely and angry child, with my already sensitive system now accelerated to 'Mach 3', a level far beyond my ability to manage or control. By chance, at the age of ten years I discovered the benefit and buzz of long-distance running, and for the next 50 years used this as a daily means of burning off the enormous amount of excess energy that my damaged neuro-system generated.

I am still the sort of person whose eyes are constantly moving from one thing to another, whose hands are never still, and I very seldom ever sit — let alone sit still! Even now, at 70-plus years of age I still regard myself as a 'high energy person', but definitely not 'hyperactive'.

At this stage of my life, I happily acknowledge that without my elevated levels of energy I would never have achieved some of the more worthwhile aspects of my life, and now finally, in my retirement years, I am managing to assert some degree of control over my body and its energy.

Yes, I am a high-energy person, but contrary to what the label ADHD suggests, I do not have difficulty in paying attention, and I don't have an attention deficit.

No, but I do have an attention-*overdose* difficulty. I pay attention to everything my sensory system detects. Although this is hard for other people to tolerate, it does not exhaust me, but it does mean that I am dealing with a huge amount of sensory input, and this can be extremely confusing. Whereas most people are able to self-protect by shutting down much of their extraneous sensory responsiveness and focusing primarily on what is central to them at that moment, I do not have the ability to consciously or unconsciously control my responsiveness in this way.

It could well be argued that my style is maladaptive and antisocial in our largely predator-free city living, and that it is perhaps a remnant of a lifestyle more akin to a cave-dwelling tribe, where my skills and talents would be invaluable in a whole range of social functions such as hunting and protection from predators. However, when you put me in a modern-day classroom with 30 other children, ask me to sit still and listen, listen, listen, then my receptors become overloaded, bombarded with hundreds of signals that I cannot mute, and I have difficulty coping, often feeling as if I am about to explode.

So, if we really understood what is going on for these children, and if we really wanted to find a useful descriptor, we could label them as AOD — 'attention overload difficulty' — which has *very* different implications from the ADHD label.

The label impacts the adult as well as the child

The real point here is that when we accept a label, we implicitly accept that it is appropriate — that the label fits the child — and the child 'fits' the label. We tag the child with a convenient label, valid or not valid, then try to problem-solve via that understanding of the child.

The danger here is that we inadvertently respond according to our understanding of that label, and in doing so we may be stereotyping the child in an erroneous and harmful manner. This is particularly the case when we start using 'medications' to try to 'fix' the child.

But there is more. For a very high proportion of these dyslexic children, not only are the child's external physical senses hypervigilant in the way described above, but so also is their whole nutritional and sensory system — and this is where the H (hyperactivity) element arises.

Over the last 40 years the commercial production of our daily food has become more and more controlled by the ethics and motivations of the commercial producers and their accountants. In the early 1950s when I was a child my family grew almost all of our food — vegetables, fruit and meat. Very little of what I ate was mass produced and almost none of it contained additives of any nature, until Jungle Juice came along.

Things have changed completely now and children's bodies are being bombarded by foreign chemicals via foods, fluids and even shampoos, toothpaste and laundry products. Add a cocktail of electrical and electronic radiation, toxic fumes and spray-drift, and we have created a pollution-filled human body that starts to break down in a variety of ways — colds, the flu, nervous twitches, sleep difficulties, depression, anxiety and, of course, cancer.

Over time the commercial interests have gained almost free rein in their methods of processing our taste-enhanced, long-life, pre-packaged foods, assuring us that the chemical additives will not harm us, while the pharmaceutical companies create chemical remedies that will prevent or mask assorted health difficulties, and even correct the so-called 'chemical imbalance in our brain' — while making huge financial profit for themselves. (It is interesting to note that there is absolutely no scientific evidence to support the notion that psychiatric disturbance is the product of a 'chemical imbalance in the brain', and it is my understanding that this catchphrase was actually invented by a journalist working for one of the pharmaceutical companies! The only time there is a 'chemical imbalance in the brain' is when we ingest something — usually in tablet form — that puts it there!)

Hyperactivity

In my long experience as a child and family psychologist I saw hundreds of children referred as potentially 'hyperactive'. Of these only two were really hyperactive. Yes, most of the others were driving their parents nuts with their erratic and unpredictable behaviour, but (in my opinion) only after the parents had driven the kids nuts, by using 'rules, reward and punishment' discipline and control systems that left the kids totally bewildered and confused. And that is completely aside from the impact of all the 'go faster' foods!

Elsewhere in this book I explain the difficulty 'diesel' children have with rules or requests that have no pictorial content ('hurry up', 'come here', 'behave yourself', 'tidy up' and the like) and the anxiety and distress that this can generate. The parents see the child as being uncooperative and rebellious, but from the child's point of view the parents are demanding, unpredictable, intolerant and unfair, often ranting and raving, and sometimes even violent. In such a scenario TLC can become a diluted commodity.

When we add in the cumulative impact of food additives, commercial chemicals and pollution, as well as a huge variety of electrical radiation, we commonly end up with a child who cannot cope and whose behaviour can become quite extreme.

When these children are brought to see me, they have usually already been 'tagged' — and the popular tag these days seems to be ADHD. Indeed, it seems that in North America this tag seems to be used interchangeably with 'dyslexia', adding further evidence to support the notion that the people tagging the children with these labels have little understanding of what either label really involves.

Understandably, the parents want help, and the children need to be rescued. What isn't helpful is that so often they have been led to believe that the help they all need comes in the form of a little white pill called Ritalin.

Ritalin

At this stage my professional ethics call for me to declare that I am an anti-drug operator, and I can see no benefit from putting chemicals into the brains of children and adults alike in order to moderate or modify behaviour we are not comfortable with. I know this is an unpopular stance, but in all my years of practice, I have met only one child who told me he genuinely felt that Ritalin was a beneficial and worthwhile adjunct to his childhood.

It is ironic that when we as adults have problems coping with a child or some aspect of their behaviour, we call that child a 'problem child'. We have a problem in that we don't like the child's behaviour, so we label the child as having a problem. This term really only says that we don't understand what is going on for that child, and that we don't know how to help that child. Our own confusion as teachers or parents is not legitimate reason for us to put poisonous chemicals into the brains of our children in order for us to feel that we have some control of the situation.

Psychology still has a long way to go in our endeavours to really understand the human brain and individual behaviour and, like medicine, a long way to go to free itself from the polluting dynamics of commerce and the all-governing profit-driven manifesto.

So, what is ADHD really?

'Hyperactivity' means very high levels of activity, as opposed to 'hypo-activity' which means just the opposite.

The hyperactive child is more than just an intensively active child. This child moves at an unbelievable rate, is generally erratically spontaneous, and moves constantly and intrusively into and through everything. They recognize few barriers and no bruised sensitivities — nothing is out of bounds as far as their inquisitiveness is concerned. They will commonly have an explosive start to the day — eclipsing the local rooster — and will move like a turbo-charged maniac until dropping in their tracks sometime short of midnight.

Although many children are labelled 'hyperactive', few really fit the bill — and for this we should be very grateful.

More often we have children who, although excessively active, do not warrant the title 'hyperactive' and certainly do not warrant medication. They do, however, deserve support and assistance, and an investigation of the possible dynamics that might be causing a lifestyle that is as uncomfortable for them as it is for those sharing their living space.

Many children who fall under the descriptor 'dyslexic' present as having heightened sensitivity to a multitude of environmental factors, which can individually or as a group create a stressed neuro/muscular system. Identification and monitoring of these environmental factors can bring huge relief to all concerned. Typically, chemicals, minerals and electrical current are the main culprits.

The sustained physical function of the human body can be seen as a product of a harmonious interaction of two major physiological systems — one being chemical, and the other electrical — together being major factors in our neurological functioning. Each individual person has slightly differing needs in terms of their chemical and mineral resources, and any maladjustment (under or over) has the capacity to impact on the way the individual nervous system will operate.

As with motor vehicles, some people are highly tuned, and hence highly vulnerable to variation within their system, and others are so low-tuned that nothing seems to impact on their performance at all. Too much or too little of anything, ranging from trace elements, through vitamins, minerals, proteins, sugars, to foreign chemicals (as in preservatives, flavouring chemicals and the like), to foreign electrical impulses or force fields can push a child well beyond their own ability to cope.

Chemicals and minerals

While our bodies absolutely depend on the presence of various chemicals and minerals in varying amounts, some are foreign to our needs and can have a cumulatively poisoning effect. Foreign chemicals and minerals can enter our body in a number of ways:

- They can be entirely natural and be present in our natural foods (salicylates in apples, feijoas and tomato sauce, for example).
- They can be natural but be presented in unnatural ways (dried fruits having a changed sugar form or squeezed juices having sugar concentrates out of balance from that of the raw fruit).
- They can be natural, but not naturally in our food chain (chlorine and fluoride in our town drinking water, zinc in sunburn prevention cream, or lead in steel packaging).

They can equally be present as part of our food preparation process (chemicals used to wash carrots and potatoes or to ripen bananas), or be remnant from cleaning processes (chlorine in cleaners), or be present as additives to preserve, colour, flavour and 'stabilize' our food. (Your local naturopath or nutritionist could tell you much more about this.)

As part of their heightened sensitivity, many ADHD (perhaps that should now be AOHD) children will present as having food allergies, or at least food intolerances, with dairy and wheat products (gluten) perhaps being the two most commonly identified.

We frequent our supermarkets and buy our foods in good faith, with a predominant attitude that 'they wouldn't sell it to us if it wasn't good for us'. Few people stop to consider the poisons they regularly put into their own body — or actively provide for their children — under the guise of 'food'. Few consumers realize that the sulphides and sulphates that are a common ingredient in our canned and bottled drinks act like a brick on the body's accelerator, and bolt-cutters through the brake cable, producing what is arguably the first significant, chemically induced, mind-altering experience in the young child's life. Have another Coke, feel refreshed!

Electrical

And then there is the electrical side of our mechanism — incorporating the entire nervous system.

That our modern lifestyle involves a multitude of electrical and electronic gadgetry is readily recognized, but what of the impact of electrical radiation?

Consider the battery in your wristwatch, and the radiation from your smart phone, your kitchen microwave, TV and computer or the alarm/radio beside the bed. What of the ever-present current from your electric blanket (even though it is turned off), your home meter-board (Smart Meters), and the sub-station or transformer on the street. What about stray radiation from the local phone tower and microwave relay station? All of these may be draining your own energy, and wreaking havoc with the delicate internal balance of your child, making it impossible for them to regulate their activity or behaviour.

In my work as an educational psychologist, when asked to work with a child with behavioural difficulties, my first intervention was often to simply remove the child's wristwatch and cellphone (electrical radiation?) for two weeks. With some children this was all I needed to do.

Considering this, is it at all appropriate for you to berate your child, or to punish them or to medicate them in an attempt to change their behaviour — to punish them for something that might be well beyond their knowledge or control?

Medication?

Is it useful or wise to medicate your child, and in doing so add yet another chemical ingredient to the environmental cocktail of poisons they might be experiencing, in order to calm and regulate them, and do you include these in the 'must be good for us' category? We now live in a society where medical wisdom sometimes operates on the basis of prescribing medications to simply *remove symptoms*. The huge growth of 'over the counter' medications testifies to this.

As a parent and 'hyperactive' child who has become a highly energetic adult, I urge for a responsible examination of all the possible dynamics of each individual child by those primarily charged with their safe-keeping — you, the parents.

As parents, surely it is our responsibility to take charge of the child's environment, so they can readily take charge of their own behaviour.

This, and other related approaches, feature as a central theme in my parenting manual: *With, Not Against* (2008).

(There is a delightful photo-based children's book by Kathy Hoopmann entitled *All Dogs Have ADHD* (2008) that presents a refreshing perspective on this 'condition'.)

In the next chapter we take a more positive stance and examine how the 'diesel/dyslexic' style can be advantageous in our work life.

> **In dealing with dyslexia we must avoid the temptation to 'adjust' or otherwise change the natural style of the student. In these situations, our energies must be focused on the beliefs and processes of the teaching staff.**

Chapter Seven
Benefits of dyslexia

Yes, the 'diesel/dyslexic' style has an upside, and we owe it to the children to teach them that their style has been and will continue to be central to the development of our physical and social world.

- Are there any benefits from being dyslexic?
- Some advantages

Are there any benefits from being dyslexic?

Because of the basic difference in their thinking style, and the consequent confusion and failure in their early lives, 'dyslexics' tend to be prone to periods of depression and general low self-concept. They often feel that they are 'not good enough', and they live with a fear of rejection. Knowledge and information for parents and school teachers has, to date, been so inadequate that it has been almost standard that the dyslexic child has been poorly understood by the adults around them. More than this, their difficulty in the education system means that they have less understanding of the academic world, experience failure in that context, and have often been directly or indirectly blamed for their own failure. The predictable consequence of such a start to life is a fragile self-concept, and a marked tendency to depression — the product of feeling out of control of everything in one's life.

To finally get recognition of their dyslexia as a lifelong affliction is a major relief to many adults. It allows them to finally know that there is a recognized cause behind their confusion and difficulty. But really, in itself, this doesn't fix anything. As one young man rather cynically asked me, 'Ha, I'm dyslexic — so which pill do I take?' We have to recognize that this sense of relief in itself does nothing to change their lifelong, overriding sense of failure and anger.

Ron Davis, in his handbook *The Gift of Dyslexia* (2010), sympathetically attempts to reframe the dyslexic state as a gift (as opposed to the curse that so many of us experience). Personally, I find it almost insulting to dismiss dyslexia as a 'gift', but in keeping with Ron's positive initiative we continue the exercise here by way of an exploration of the upside of the pictorial, non-linguistic thinking style.

Carrying a range of what we may call 'diesel' personal characteristics, adult male 'dyslexics' have historically been drawn to such employment roles as manual labourers, drivers, tradesmen, mechanics, engineers, architects and artists, or to work with animals. To some degree they have often gravitated to this style of employment as a result of lack of higher educational achievement, but also because of their hands-on, creative, pictorial skill style. The IT, entertainment and hospitality industries currently have a similar draw to school-leaving 'dyslexics'. On the other hand, sadly our prisons become eventual host to a disproportionately high percentage of our male dyslexic population (by one calculation a whopping 84 per cent of male prisoners are dyslexic!), who retain the usual personal achievement goals of society but lack the legitimate means to achieve them.

While the term dyslexia refers to a restricted capacity for

language, arguably the reality of the dyslexic state is more a natural inclination to think in pictures. As our educational and assessment systems are essentially language-based, the lack of word sense is a marked disadvantage in childhood. But as the person grows beyond the grasp of the education system the hands-on, pictorial thinking style can come into its own and provide some marked advantages over non-pictorial persons.

Some advantages

Practicality

Initially, it is worth noting that in a purely practical world the dyslexic person might actually be at an advantage. They are more likely (than the language thinker) to be able to rapidly visually assess and respond to demanding life situations, and therefore more likely to survive in situations of crisis or duress. On this basis it is easy therefore to postulate that right through history the dyslexic was possibly an essential operator in (or behind) any social group, a person who could be depended upon to make things work at a practical level.

It is probable that the wheel was first created by a practical, hands-on person (rather than an academic), and similarly many of the inventions that now characterize our society (building technique, cars, planes, tools, implements and so on) have been conceptualized, engineered and developed by pictorial, hands-on people — potentially the 'dyslexics' of our education system. (The internal combustion engine was invented by a Belgian blacksmith!)

Precision

Backyard engineers, innovators and inventors more often than not are pictorial thinkers. As such they carry some degree of dyslexia — as may master craftsmen and precision artisans such as watchmakers or the builders of violins. Here, as in the development of nanotechnology, the ability to visualize minute componentry, magnified many thousands of times, moving or stationary, from any perspective, and in a series of different functions, is a huge advantage and can be seen as a 'gift' associated with the dyslexic style.

Design

'Dyslexics' in particular tend to have a heightened sense of spatial arrangement, the sense of what something would look like if viewed from a range of different perspectives. This applies to any design process, be it landscaping, furniture, design or art-form. House design is a case in point, with most architects, draughtspeople and builders being able to sense the 'feel' of a house from looking at a plan — a bird's-eye drawing.

Construction

Beyond design is the actual hands-on manipulation of the materials of construction. Whether it be engineering, the fabrication of clothing, working with wood or laying concrete, the person who is able to 'feel' and 'read' their materials will have a distinct advantage over the person who just processes what is in front of them. Knowledge and insight are likely to provide advantage over those who merely rely on theoretical information. Again, this is an arena where the dyslexic operator is likely to show insights that will advance them to the front of (and even considerably ahead of) their field.

Multi-thinking

While acknowledging that on one hand the pictorial thinker is subjected to particular limitations in their thinking style, on the other hand there are benefits that come directly as a product of that thinking style.

One of the significant benefits of being dyslexic is the absence of certain constraints to thinking. Although any 'word-thinker' (i.e. 'normal' person) would not consider themselves to be particularly constrained in their thinking, they can really only think in a manner similar to this line of text that you are currently reading. That is, they think in a singular line of words (linear thinking) and can only move to a different line by ceasing the current one. In this writing I can present an idea via a string of words, but to present a different idea I must use a subsequent and different string of words.

While admittedly largely deprived of linguistic thinking, the dyslexic person is not constrained in this way and has the ability to (pictorially) think several different things at the same time. This can be likened to a closed circuit TV security centre, where several CCTV screens are viewed at once. In this, the visual operator can compare and contrast anything they can visualize, from material objects to social situations, actual or fantasy, supposed or potential. They do this by using a multiple 'split-screen' movie format in their pictorial brain, so that two or more concepts are presented simultaneously and may even be processed or advanced simultaneously in terms of their growth, wear or change over time — forwards or backwards. The potential for development of ideas, designs or concepts is almost unlimited. It was this style of thinking that allowed New Zealand's John Britten to develop and build his world-beating superbike in his Christchurch backyard, and it currently allows other similar designers and inventors to advance design and technology simultaneously.

Information load

The difference between the language (linear) thinking style, and the pictorial (dyslexic) thinking style is similar to the difference between a live radio report of a football match and the same game seen on TV. In the radio version you have only one string of words informing you, while in the other, your eyes can supply you with a much wider range of information simultaneously — any part of the play, from any part of your screen.

However, as in many situations, along with the benefit there is an associated difficulty. The downside here is the complication involved in mentally processing so much information at once, or in answering the simple question 'What are you thinking?'. Davis (2010) suggests that the dyslexic person can have up to 60,000 units of information in their thinking space at any one moment. No wonder they sometimes look a little overwhelmed and dreamy — and the typical answer to the above question is, 'Um, nothing' — which is so far from the truth but gets them off the hook of trying to explain in words.

Animal husbandry

It has long been recognized that the human being stands apart from other animals on the basis of our use of language as a thinking tool. Such a statement, however, distracts us from crediting animals with any real thinking skills at all. Those who work closely with animals will quickly assert that animals do think, do communicate with each other via thought, and can readily exchange thoughts with humans — sending and receiving messages via *picture thought*. Dogs and horses are particularly good at this, as it would appear that pictorial processing is a key thinking tool for them. This is an arena where 'dyslexics' shine. Vets, animal trainers, drovers, competitive horse riders and others are commonly pictorial thinkers. In working with humans, however, 'diesels' do benefit from being with a person who similarly thinks in pictures and is prepared and able to readily join in the exchange.

Visualization

A wide range of professions rely on visualization and creative visualization. The surgeon handling tiny elements of tissue they cannot directly see, the computer tech talking a client through repairs by phone, a weather forecaster, plumber or mechanic assessing a problem they cannot physically see, all depend to a large degree on their ability to formulate useful pictures of the unseen situation, within their own mind.

The advertising guru, the fantasy writer, the film writer, director and editor must all be able to create and hold specific pictorial representations in their brain while then manipulating and processing them in a number of possible directions at once — not at all possible without finely developed pictorial-thinking ability.

Machine operation

A combination of the 'hands-on', the visual and the engineering skills can create the precision skills basic to safe and efficient machine operation. Whether it be digger-driving, logging operations, forestry arborist work, heavy machine operation, explosives work or commercial passenger work (road, air or water transport), the combination of skills required here falls directly into the realm and style of the hands-on, practical dyslexic-style person.

The practical person

Having a natural inclination to be a pictorial thinker and a hands-on operator, the dyslexic person can be seen as being a 'must include' in any project team, be it setting up the campsite, or keeping the precision-engineering manufacturing complex humming or coordinating underground mining. This person so often demonstrates the ability to visually assess a situation, immediately understand exactly what needs to be done, in what sequence, then does it there and then with no fuss, no bother and no disruption. That they cannot verbally explain what they are doing should not be allowed to be a hindrance — they should be allowed to just get out there and do it, alone if need be. Their track record will demonstrate the level of freedom they should be accorded here.

The professional problem-solver

Imagine being able to slow a movie down, to run it forwards, backwards, and to be able to simultaneously run several alternative 'takes' at any one moment. Imagine being able to stop the movie at a difficult point, jump a period of time, see the necessary outcome, then in a series of reverse steps create the problem-solving pieces to fill in the gaps. This is one of the classic skills of the pictorial thinker — the dyslexic, the 'diesel thinker'. Rather than focusing on problems and trying to solve them, this person is often able to leap ahead of the problem, see the eventual solution as a future event, then work backwards to establish the series of steps that therefore need to be taken.

During the Second World War, English scientist and engineer Barnes Wallis demonstrated the use of such 'backwards thinking' in devising the eventual process used to effectively bounce bombs across the water surface at a calculated height and speed so that they finally sank and detonated against the inner wall of a German dam. The legend of the Dam Busters was thus established, and Wallis's experiments skipping marbles across water tanks in his garden helped determine the outcome of the war.

Alone

By definition, the dyslexic person has difficulty with language. Herein lies a problem. While they may have very highly developed constructions and visual understandings of their pet projects, communicating these usefully to other people may be very difficult for them. *Theorists* prefer to express, develop and to link their thinking via language, but *visionaries* may be quietly absorbed in their own picture show and have few useful ways of sharing this or making their ideas overt. The frustrations involved in sharing their ideas may be one of the reasons that many 'dyslexics' often work alone — and take their ideas with them when they finally depart. The inventor Nikola Tesla was quite probably one of these.

Intuition

Many dyslexic people experience themselves to be highly intuitive and may not understand their own ability to simply 'know' things. Once they learn to accept this as a natural and valued adjunct to their personal resource kit, it can greatly facilitate their thinking and their successful outcomes.

Sport

Although some 'dyslexics' are seen to be clumsy and poorly coordinated (dyspraxia), there is a notable tendency for others to achieve top-level skill in sports requiring a combination of hand–eye coordination, predictive ability and full-body reflex ability. These lucky individuals seem to have an innate ability to perceive movement, space and time in an almost intuitive manner that allows them to attain remarkable performance levels in their chosen field — be it sport or otherwise. Top performers in motocross racing, rally-sport, ice-hockey goal-keeping and America's Cup yacht racing immediately come to mind as examples.

This list could go on and on — and probably needs to if we are to adequately encourage our 'dyslexics' and confirm for them that their style is valid and valued, and that there is a place in our society for them. Without such insightful support the dyslexic person is likely to remain very vulnerable to low-level but very invasive fear.

A dyslexic person, be they adult or child, lives with dyslexia as a daily life issue. It is a thinking style that permeates virtually every aspect of life, and if not recognized as such stands to diminish a person's self-concept and severely limit their social interaction and satisfaction.

If we view dyslexia as only a reading and writing problem we effectively deny the main, submerged, bulk of the dyslexic iceberg, and we serve to cheat any dyslexic students we work with of a full satisfying life.

The next chapter endeavours to explore dyslexia as a daily life issue, and we begin by focusing on the essence of our social interaction — verbal language.

Chapter Eight
Verbal language

This chapter draws the reader's attention to the essence of the dyslexic difficulty: the prime vehicle of interaction, social communication and education across the planet — verbal language.

- The language of the dyslexic person
- Mastery
- Style
- Pictorial thinking
- Speech impediments
- Vocabulary

The language of the dyslexic person

While most authorities treat dyslexia as being a 'reading and writing' problem, here we look at the bigger picture, and see dyslexia as emanating from a style of thinking characterized by pictures rather than words. Although a dyslexic person might be able to read, write and speak to some degree, typically language is an area of confusion and difficulty for them and any social activity that depends on language may be problematic to them. If, as parents and teachers, we have some understanding of the child's difficulties, and their style with language, we are more likely to understand them better, to be more tolerant of them and, as a result, be more able to support them.

However, the specific intermeshing of dynamics that create the state of dyslexia that any one individual dyslexic will present will be unique. Each person will be different, and through this book I have explained the complexities of this. It is important to remember that no generalized description of 'typical dyslexic language' will be fully complete, or fully accurate, but some insights will assist us in our efforts to support this child.

In essence, the dyslexic child has a mind full of picture-shows, and we must remember that in most cases (despite what might seem to be overt evidence to the contrary), verbal language, as both a thinking tool and a means of expression, is not their thing.

There are a number of styles that characterize the way the dyslexic child speaks — ranging from as little as possible, to the absolute opposite of seeming to never stop talking. What is important to note here is that their manner of speaking is a reflection of the way they think.

Mastery

For a child growing up within a specific culture, with a specific language, they will generally be about twelve years old before they are considered to have mastery in terms of eloquence, structure and vocabulary. A brief (and simplistic) examination of the process of speaking, and effectively communicating, will throw light on how difficult this task can be.

Speaking aloud involves steps that most of us have learned to do automatically, and all of which may cause the dyslexic to stumble.

- Prior to any speech is an internal sense or feeling associated with a thought in our mind. That thought might be in word form, but in the dyslexic it is most likely to be in picture form.

- In selecting words to represent that thought, we clarify it internally, then select words from our available vocabulary (which may be extensive or not) that are calculated to communicate that thought to a particular listener. (This also involves recognition and presumption of the listener's relevant vocabulary.)

- These words then need to be mentally sequenced, prior to being clearly pronounced through a coordinated series of muscle movements of the lips, tongue and mouth.

- Kate Burridge in her book *Blooming English* (2002) suggests that there are 44 distinctive sounds that we must learn to make in speaking the English language, then selectively organize into syllables, which in themselves can make up hundreds of meaningful segments of words — of which the English language has about one million.

- Somewhere in this complicated process is the dynamic of breath and volume control, which results in tone, emphasis, pace, pauses and accent, all of which can dramatically alter the meaning of the sentence.

- Beyond this again is a basic understanding of nouns, verbs, adjectives and so on (the mechanical structure of the language) and their appropriate placement and use within the spoken sentence.

Spoken language is thus a remarkably complex process for any growing child to master, but even more difficult for the dyslexic child than most.

Style

Faced with such difficulty, there is little wonder that many 'dyslexics' choose to remain silent. When they do speak, or are forced to communicate verbally, the embarrassment from their errors will so often confirm for them the safety of silence. This lack of willingness or ability to express themselves has a direct impact on their social skills, their social involvement, their social success, and on their self-perception. The child will often feel inadequate, and this becomes a self-perpetuating dynamic. Most 'dyslexics' live a life dominated by such fears.

But while some choose to remain silent, others will have a huge need to share the excitement and complexity of their creative and perceptive mind — but will be frustrated by the transience of thoughts not caught immediately in verbal form. Their speed of speech (matching that of the flow of pictures in their mind) and clumsiness in articulation will predictably frustrate their listeners — and then themselves — and anger, resentment and depression may be the result. Our request for them to slow down may be potentially helpful to us, but not to them as it causes them to lose track of the passing torrent of visual thoughts. They lose track of what they wanted to say, the desired communication is thwarted, and their sense of inadequacy is confirmed.

This dynamic also lies behind the spontaneous style these children have, shouting out in class or interrupting while others are talking — they simply cannot wait, as the movie in their head is unstoppable, and they easily lose the pictures that lie behind the contribution they want to make. When the picture is gone, so too is their comment and they simply cannot remember. Our light-hearted suggestion to them that it cannot have been important, or that 'it must have been a lie' is emotionally crushing for this child.

As a result, they may speak far too fast, trying to do justice to the multitude of moving visual images in their head, and speak largely in descriptive language — without nouns. Names of people and of things may elude them, and they may well resort to descriptive language in order to identify their subject. At the same time, it is often the case that the style of their internal 'picture show' will simply preclude the use of words, and they cannot begin to give it description.

The language style of these children is often rapid, but stilted, with stops and starts, and is characteristically disjointed to the point of total confusion:

'It's like, it's got, you know, uh, like wheels, like, cos, and round, yeah round, and they like go, you know, go round.'

In others, a prime characteristic is that each sentence remains unfinished, and is superseded by a new sentence which has a different angle of attack on the same topic. But this sentence itself will remain unfinished, and be superseded by yet another, from yet a different angle or perspective:

'Yes, when I got there I wanted to … well, if I had thought of it at the time I might have … you know, they didn't even expect someone like me … but sometimes, you know, it's not worth the risk …'

— leaving the listener guessing as to what, on a better day, the conversation might have been about.

Yet others will give no hint of any verbal dysfluency or apparent difficulty with language at all. More often these are particularly intelligent 'dyslexics' who use sheer intellectual muscle to strategize and mask their areas of difficulty. They will seldom let on how hard they have to work just to appear average and 'normal'.

In some children the dyslexic style presents in their being unable to remember nouns, or other more complex words unless, or until, they can get the relevant picture (either of the object or of the word itself) to appear on their inner screen. The author is simply unable to remember the names of his own children or his own siblings, unless he can bring their names up on his internal screen — a difficulty that tends to occur in situations of tension and anxiety. This has huge capacity to stress certain relationships, as well as a person's own self-concept!

Pictorial thinking

Some adult 'dyslexics' identify not one but several 'video screens' in their mind's eye, each of which may simultaneously be presenting on quite different topics. When asked 'What are you thinking about?' — a perfectly legitimate question — their first task is to assess the focus of each 'screen', and then choose which to comment on. Which of their multiple screens will they pay attention to at any particular point, and which will they share with a particular listener? Older 'dyslexics' will often (unconsciously) quickly appraise the complex presentation on each of their screens, recoil at the thought of attempting to put meaningful words to this moving mass of information, and simply reply, 'Nothing.'

It is important to note at this point that these same picture screens are the mechanism the pictorial thinker uses for memory, and that they may well have a very accurate and extensive pictorial memory but a very poor verbal memory. This pictorial memory is often mistaken for 'long-term' memory, and the (lack of) verbal memory for poor short-term memory — or, accusingly, of a lack of interest!

Experience has demonstrated that it is seldom useful to ask a dyslexic child, 'Do you think in pictures?' Inevitably, they will look confused and answer, 'No', while giving you full evidence via their eye, head and hand movements (as well as their visually descriptive language) that this is exactly what they do. From their point of view, they just think, and they have never considered how they do this, nor that they may do this differently from other people.

Some older 'dyslexics' speak in spasmodic bursts, as a product of the way the words come to them. This is one example of the use of a strategy to facilitate verbal language but where the strategy is, in itself, unreliable. For these people, some or all of the words to speak must first appear in visual form on their screen.

In one client's words:

'When I'm stressed or upset I see the words coming out of a sausage-machine in my mind. The harder and the longer words take longer to come out of the word-tube, and sometimes I have to wait to be able to see what the word is — it's a bit like karaoke, but my words move like a stream across my screen.'

With this man, the difficulty was compounded by the fact that the words appeared from his right, with the latter end of the word taking time to appear, so making it difficult to even begin to guess what the whole word might be. Brief consideration of this difficulty would suggest a real trap with words that have alternative endings and may go some way to explain the frequent malapropisms and spoonerisms typical of the dyslexic speaker. Is it *poly ur ... ethene or inate?*

Speech impediments

A lisp, a stutter, an r/w confusion (real/weal) and/or a th/f confusion (three/free) are common in the dyslexic speaker'. With these 'speech impediments' we need to be very careful that our 'assistance' does not further penalize the child (receiving 'help' means that you are not doing well enough — that you are failing) and we need to be aware that our 'motivational' comments such as 'stop this baby-talk' can be hugely destructive.

With children who have a th/f or r/w confusion, it might be useful to avoid correcting their speech, but instead help them build up the appropriate muscular skills by getting a parent to take the child's hands each morning before breakfast, and slowly and clearly, three times, say together 'Three, thick, things', and 'No worry, no cry'. Exercise the speech muscles this way, first thing each morning, and allow the child to progressively implement the skills in their speech through the day when and as they can.

Your local speech and language therapist will also be able to help directly or give you tips, but as with any remedial help programme, take your cue from the child. If the child is enjoying the assistance and attends willingly, keep it up. However, if the child resists and resents the 'help', be very careful of backfire and damage to their self-concept.

Vocabulary

Finally, on a preventative note, it is highly recommended that right from birth (or even before) we minimize the volume and use of TV, radio and hi-fi in the household — and maximize the amount of talking we do with the child. Although for the first few years this will be a one-way conversation (*'Now we will just pop you up here on the bench, while I put the plug in, in this little hole here, and turn on the tap, and then we'll get the dishes done. A wee squirt of this stuff here — see the bubbles coming…*), this will have the effect of exposing the child to a wide variety of language. It will normalize spoken language as an interpersonal activity, and it will implant a wide vocabulary in the child. By doing this we stand to extend the word-toolbox that the child will have in their head when they arrive at school — probably the single most useful educational lift you could give any child.

This deliberately extended vocabulary will be available to the child as an overt communication tool. These words will allow them greater participation in a wide range of conversations, which in turn will provide them with more social and mental stimulation. Such an extended vocabulary will also allow the child to grasp and understand more complex teachings, as well as to process and express themselves in the educational context.

Beyond this increased overt use of language, an extended vocabulary is also available to the child (dyslexic or not) as an internal thinking tool for their own use in processing ideas, thoughts and perceptions, and in extending these via comparisons and conjecture, as well as remembering things they have been told.

In terms of parental input and direct parental contribution to a child's success in school, satisfaction in social interaction and future elevation in the workforce, the simple exercise of deliberately talking with your young child as much as possible, thereby extending their use of language as much as possible, is arguably one of the most significant contributions a parent can make to a child's current — and future — life.

Verbal language can be regarded as a release or freeing agent for the interactive human being. Without language we remain significantly restricted in our ability to recognize our own perceptions, to process them and to use them as a currency of social interaction. The less language we have at our disposal, the more prone we are to loneliness, frustration and eventual depression — and the growth of antisocial attitudes — and that is where we will take our focus next.

> **We must persistently remind ourselves that any 'help' given to a struggling student is an operation of the two-edged sword: 'what you currently are is not good enough'.**

Chapter Nine
Family and home

In this and the following chapter, we bring our focus back to the private and personal world of the child — to reveal how deeply they can be injured as a product of the misunderstandings on the part of the important adults in their life.

At this stage of our exploration, the reader may find significance in the current rise in educational disengagement, social aggression, gang behaviour, prison population and firearms offences in marginalized groups, with the observed commonality of poor school achievement.

- Frustration
- Depression
- Parenting the dyslexic child
- Pictorial thinking — how it plays out in our parenting
- Concepts of time
- Consistency, predictability and emotional security
- Empowerment and disempowerment
- Empowering the child

It is an undeniable fact that many so-called dyslexic children are bright — even *very* bright — in terms of their actual intelligence. Because of their inherent difficulties with language, this intellectual capacity might not be evident to teachers, employers or even their parents and they may rather be labelled as 'cunning', 'devious', 'unmotivated' or even 'lazy'. These labels often demonstrate a misunderstanding, an intolerance and even an active dislike of the child.

This situation is the direct product of a lack of useful information about the dyslexic condition and will predictably diminish as more useful information is made available to the educational community.

Frustration

With a more enlightened and empathetic assessment, we may see that it is often the case that the child is intelligent but severely frustrated in a number of ways. This is where an understanding of the real implications of dyslexia may help us see the child in a different light. Remembering that this child has a limited ability with language (i.e. to use words as a thinking tool; to use spoken language as a form of communication; to readily understand the implications of specific words; or to understand the phonological mechanics of written language), we may start to recognize the range and depth of their frustration.

It is predictable that:

- They cannot articulate their thinking and so cannot communicate their intelligence in an interactive way.
- They cannot make their ideas, wants and needs known, so cannot achieve what they would like to achieve.

- Their attempts are often misinterpreted by others and in this they are short-changed at a personal level.
- In being unable to interact meaningfully they are also unable to advance their thinking through interaction with their intellectual peers.
- Their thoughts remain trapped in pictorial and emotional form within them, and they are unable to even process and clarify them within their own thinking as this process is typically enhanced via the use of an internal language thought-train — something they are unable to do.
- They are denied permission by authority persons (parents, teachers, employers, bosses) to demonstrate their real capability, and their attempts to achieve this are met with a range of derisive and restrictive responses.
- They are constantly subjected to directives, instruction and discussion that is aimed at their *apparent* intelligence level, and as such it is demeaning and insulting to them.
- They are unable to negotiate decisions, outcomes and processes with authority persons (who may be intellectually less able than themselves) and so have to endure slow or restrictive situations which they know are unnecessary.

(Note that all these factors of frustration are equally experienced by the adult who suffers a debilitating (left-side) stroke that affects their language ability, as well as by members of the congenitally deaf community.)

In effect, these situations put 'dyslexics' in a situation of huge frustration, where they are effectively out of control of their own outcomes. They cannot achieve things they know they are fully capable of achieving and desperately want to achieve, and they cannot demonstrate these capabilities to others.

Being 'out of control of your own desired outcomes' is, in the opinion of this writer, the essence of the emotional state that we call *depression*.

If this is correct, taking a pill for your depression is counter-productive, a waste of time and needless poisoning of your body and brain.

The combination of being both dyslexic and intellectually astute can thus be akin to mental torture. The dyslexic person experiences severe frustration and herein lies yet another problem. Whereas the language-thinking person has the capacity to internally process their situation, recognize the characteristics of frustration, and verbalize this to important others — therapist, counsellor, parent ('Mum, it is so frustrating when the history teacher will only see it from one point of view.') — our dyslexic cannot. They cannot rationalize, let alone communicate and share their emotional state in this way, feel stymied at an emotional level, and eventually express their frustration in the only way they can — via abrupt and expressive physical action.

This physical expression is typically seen as one of *anger*. And so here the situation compounds yet again and the child is labelled as 'angry' (a self-fulfilling label) and sometimes even 'violent'.

These labels further frustrate the child, and cause authority persons to take a negative and disciplinary reaction to them, and we have a self-propelling, downwards spiral. The child stands to be branded by teachers and classmates as being a behaviour problem, and may become the target of 'preventative discipline', and the self-fulfilling negative cycle continues. All too often the child eventually accepts the reputation and becomes the angry, conflictual person others believe them to be.

Today we live with a growing body of discontented, antisocial, aggressive men who carry high levels of frustration and negativity generated in the experiences of failure in their early schooling.

Depression

Fortunately, not all of these children accept the 'anger' label, and many can clearly see that accepting such a label (and the associated status) is not going to be to their own advantage. But what other options do they have? Very few — and so many simply become resigned to their position, accept this as the reality of their life and become *depressed*. They are out of control of their desired outcomes, their active options will clearly just make things worse, and they sink back into a non-state — a passive state of depression.

CONSTRAINED
RESTRICTED
ACCUSED
NOT IN CONTROL
DEPRESSED

At this point the 'system' typically springs into action. Well-meaning people see the recognizable symptoms of depression (but perhaps not the realities of the situation), worry about possible undesirable outcomes, and come forth with medication designed to alleviate the symptoms. Many people, including very young children and 'dyslexics', are inappropriately medicated on the basis of such depression.

Medication, although historically mainly herbal in essence, is currently more often than not based on proprietary drugs — a mixture of chemicals and minerals designed to stimulate or suppress specific elements of our natural system. This topic was given some attention in Chapter Six, examining the notions of ADD and ADHD.

Although for many the lifestyle associated with being dyslexic is painful and limited, with insightful support the positive attributes of dyslexia can be experienced and selectively enhanced.

In summary, it would be forgivable to believe that the dyslexic community is a significant section of our society that is actively damned by the selective overuse of our greatest asset — language — in the education of our young. A quick look at the prison statistics of most (if not all) western societies is indeed sobering:

- An extremely high proportion of our prisoners are male.
- The literacy rate in our prisons is extraordinarily low.
- Over 60 per cent of the prison population favour their left hand.
- Over 80 per cent of prisoners (in New Zealand, for example, according to the Dyslexia Foundation of New Zealand) have been diagnosed as dyslexic.

Parenting the dyslexic child

Parenting a dyslexic child can be a lonely and, in some cases, even an emotionally devastating experience. Not complying readily with the rules of childhood, the dyslexic child can be unpredictable, unfathomable, incorrigible and intolerable. 'Normal' parenting strategies tend to work once, but only once, with these children, and many parents find themselves tempted to become more and more heavy-handed in their desperate need to assert some sort of control over this errant family member.

Not doing what they have been told to do, doing what they have been specifically told not to do (or have just been punished for doing!), looking angelic when guilt and grief is the order of the day, these children just don't make sense, and repeated punishment has no useful impact.

Fear of pain, fear of loss and fear of being caught do seem to work as 'disciplinary' mechanisms, to a degree. Unfortunately, they also tend to generate resentment, fear and deviousness in the child, and a certain resilience against the impact of punishment. Few parents are likely to enjoy hitting a child, but for those who resort to it, the question is often simply: 'How else can I control my child?'

In this dilemma some parents revert to an unfortunate human tendency of when something does not work, doing it again, louder, harder, faster — as if under the belief that a more extreme version will be more effective than what has been done before.

Although some parental requests for assistance may be initially related to the dyslexic child's learning style and needs, more commonly when parents ask for help, their concern relates to the child's *behaviour* and their request is for techniques of control.

Although my earlier book *With, Not Against* (King 2008) is a parenting manual designed to assist all parents and all children, it is particularly applicable in situations where the child is dyslexic. In essence this book differs from most in that rather than assisting parents to *control children*, the approach presented is to assist parents to understand and *control their own input* in such a manner that their children are able to easily cooperate and give the parents the behaviour they are looking for. In this we leave the child in control of their own behaviour — and it works.

For a full and practical presentation of the language of parenting — how to instruct children and how to talk with them — the reader is referred to this earlier publication. Below, however, we present a brief overview of the reasons for using a certain style of language with dyslexic children.

Pictorial thinking — how it plays out in our parenting

In the case of the dyslexic child there are certain characteristics which parents would benefit from understanding. The most significant of these is based in the way we think.

As we have seen, dyslexic children (and many non-dyslexic children, especially boys) think in pictures. We must accept this as a prevailing dynamic. Accept it, and work with it. What this means is that in order to be effective in our communication with them, we have to give them the pictures that go *with* our message. If our message has *no* picture, or if it puts the *wrong* picture into the child's head, *we* will have created a communication breakdown.

We too often end up with the old outcome: '*I told him not to do it, he knew he shouldn't do it, but he went ahead and did it anyway. It was deliberate!'*

Consider the message to a child *'Catch the ball'*, often shortened to just *'Catch'*. It creates a clear *picture* in our mind, usually of a person, maybe a child, reaching out with one or both hands to catch a ball. In our mind we have a picture of what we want the child to do, and the words we use somehow represent and communicate this picture — or do they?

Ideally, the words the adult uses will create the same picture — or at least their own version of it — in the mind of the child. This message is therefore a *pictorial* one, putting an image in the brain of the child, an image that helps the child to attempt the task. (This is a basic tactic used in sports psychology and in motivational workshops, and it is very effective.)

However, now consider what picture comes up in your brain when we change the *nature* of the message by phrasing it in negative terms. Our intention is the same, but our words are different. In this case as the father throws the ball to the child he says, *'Don't drop it'*. As above, a clear picture will pop up in the child's mind — but it will be a very different image, with a very different outcome. This time the picture is invariably of the child not catching but *dropping* the ball.

How does this happen? In both examples the intention of the speaker is for the child to catch the ball, but in the second example the different words create a different picture, which in turn creates a different outcome — *dropping the ball*. This picture is as hypnotically powerful as its alternative in the first example, but because of its verbal/pictorial content it will increase the chances of the child dropping the ball.

What we are saying here is that *the words create the picture, and the picture creates the outcome.*

Although we know what we mean when we say, 'Don't drop the ball', most people don't really seem to understand the impact of our words, in terms of the way the child will hear, and see, the message.

There is no picture for the command 'don't'. Sure, you can draw a picture of a circle with a slash across it, but that is a socially learned symbol, not a natural pictorial message. The child does hear 'don't', but, as is the case for many words we use, it does not create any pictorial reaction in the child's brain. The rest of the sentence still remains, and it does create a very clear picture, but of an outcome we really want to avoid.

'Catch' and 'Don't drop' are used here as examples, and in themselves are hardly significant. The significance occurs, however, when we use this style of instructional language, as in the following everyday examples:

- 'Don't spill your drink.'
- 'Don't run around corners.'
- 'Don't play with matches' — to which we often add a further (hypnotic command picture) — 'you will burn yourself.'
- 'Don't swear.'

- 'Don't touch.'
- 'Don't worry.'
- 'Don't forget.'
- 'Don't climb the trees.'
- 'Don't slam the door.'
- 'Don't push in.'
- 'Don't be late.'
- 'Don't panic.'
- 'Don't argue.'
- 'Don't tease.'
- 'Don't leave your bike on the driveway.'
- 'No shouting.'
- 'No running.'

And so we hear ourselves ranting at our children: 'How many times do I have to tell you, don't tease the cat!'

Of equal frustration to all concerned is the adult tendency to use sentences like 'If you run, you will trip and fall'. When the child unwittingly complies with this pictorial message, the parent is just as likely to add 'I told you so!' — and yet still have no understanding of their own instrumental role in this outcome.

(The interesting — and rather sad — part of this is that for many picture-thinking adults, although they understand the intention of the message, their understanding is overridden by the hypnotic impact of the pictorial aspect of the message. Thus, the person who tells their partner *You are always late* will further consolidate the partner's style of being late. To start to change this, use 'I'd love it if you were on time tonight — or even a couple of minutes early — thanks, Honey' — and enjoy the difference.)

The clear message here is that when we use language that creates a picture in the child's brain, that is what the child will act on — whether it be the one we want or not. Rather than blaming the child, it is up to us to choose words that will allow the child to give us the behaviour we want. Sorry, but this also means that as parents we need to 'engage brain before opening mouth'.

So, think of what you do want the child to do. Now choose words that will put that picture (and only that picture) into the child's brain.

But this is only half of the story. Most children (but especially boys) up to the age twelve or so are heavily pictorial in their thinking. What happens when we use language that has no useful picture?

Look at the following list of commonly used instructions and consider how many of them fail to offer a clear visual message for the child to act on at all.

Put your things away. (What is a 'thing', and what does it look like?)

Behave yourself.	*Hurry up.*	*Tidy up.*
Show more respect.	*Just relax.*	*Don't forget.*

Be more courteous.	*Help.*	*Be kind.*
Leave that alone.	*Get ready.*	*Wait.*
Come here.	*Don't even think about it.*	*Think about it.*

These are just some of the verbal instructions that we give our children, which have no clear pictorial equivalent — they cannot be drawn. You may know exactly what you want the child to do, but these instructions do not put that picture into the child's thinking. (Many parents will visualize/draw a person running for the command '*Hurry up*', but that picture in the child's mind will only come from the use of the word '*run*'.)

These instructions need to be reworded in a manner that leaves a useful pictorial message in the child's thinking. For example, '*Hurry up*' could be changed to '*run*', and '*Get ready*' could more usefully be '*Grab your bag and put your shoes on*'.

These are the children who, having been told to '*Go and tidy your bedroom*', will be found twenty minutes later, in their bedroom, playing or reading comics. The word 'bedroom' will have given them a picture of where they should be, but 'tidy' is a concept that has no particular picture, so no action follows. In fact, these children are cooperating as far as they are able — by going to their bedroom — yet still are admonished for not cooperating with the instruction. How unfair.

Similarly, in the early-morning school-day rush, predictably nothing useful will happen when we tell young Steve, '*Hurry up and clean your teeth.*' But give young Steve a useful pictorial message and see the difference: '*Steve, go clean your teeth. Run.*'

(As a matter of interest, a 'hurry' is also a small wooden box on wheels, on wooden rails, historically used by children in coal mines.)

The parent may well argue that they can draw a very clear picture of what they mean — but the word *'tidy'* is not sufficient to create this picture in the child's mind, and *'quickly'* or *'hurry up'* have no pictorial equivalent either. However, watch the cartoon series that occurs in your own visual brain when you read the next sentence sequence:

'Paul, I want you to go to your bedroom. Make your bed. Put your comics in the box on the floor — and put your school uniform in the laundry.'

This works even better when we *then* say to Paul, *'Tell me what you are going to do.'* In response, Paul now reruns the pictures we put in his head and tells us in sequence what he is going to do. In doing this he creates a pictorial and verbal self-hypnotic sequence of action statements:

'I am going to go to my bedroom, sort of make my bed, chuck my ...'

This instructional sequence is very effective and very reassuring for Paul, who is now able to see what to do, to understand and cooperate! Safe at last!

For a more in-depth examination of the language of parenting, the reader is referred to *With, Not Against*, second edition.

Concepts of time

Time is a problem to the 'diesel/dyslexic' children in just about every sense.

Initially, being pictorial thinkers, they tend to have a lot of difficulty in getting to grips with the names of the days of the week or the months of the year. When the sun comes up each morning, each day looks the same. There is nothing visual about a day that would indicate its name or its position in the week.

The implication here is that the child remains constantly confused, and unable to tell each morning whether or not a particular morning is a school day. This is just another part of their life that is beyond their understanding and control, and this adds to their tendency to confusion and depression.

The 'dog-bone' week

Many parents report that their children wake in the morning and ask if they have to go to school today. Although this is commonly interpreted as indicating that the child does not want to go to school (which is probably right), it really indicates that the child has no useful means of knowing which day-name indicates a school day and which indicates a non-school day. Somehow, we need to give children a means of making sense of the structure of a week.

While the word 'Tuesday' may have little pictorial significance to a child, a typical school week can be pictorially presented so as to clearly indicate the context and the function of Tuesday.

To assist the child in this, draw up and cut out of corrugated cardboard a shape as represented below — about 20 centimetres long. The shape is the key to the child being able to successfully differentiate between weekdays and weekends. This shape — roughly in the form of a dog-bone — is pinned to the bedroom wall. The shape highlights two weekends (the good days), one at each end of a five-day series of school days, and is deliberately designed to put a little more balance into the child's perception of the week.

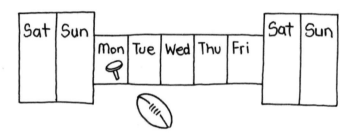

A drawing-pin or marker is placed in the current day and shifted into the next day when the child goes to bed at night. This means that the child is able to go to sleep at night knowing that the following day is a school day — or not. The child understands this from the shape of the form and can therefore differentiate a school day from a weekend day.

The child is then also able to determine how far through the week they are and can identify any special functions that may be occurring on any specific day. For example, rugby practice after school may be indicated by adding a small picture of a rugby ball under the particular day.

The same system can be used for children of separated families who may have access to the other parent on a particular schedule. In this case we might extend the model to two weeks, and by marking in those access times, allow the child some sort of understanding — a pictorial overview — of the pattern of this part of their life.

Consider what it might be like for the child who has no ability to predict what might be happening or when. For them, life would be out of control, random and scary — with depression as a likely result.

Clock time — telling the time

Now that we have sorted the days of the week, we can use a similar process to assist learning to 'tell the time'; that is, making sense of the face of a clock, and having an idea of what notions such as 'two-thirty' mean. Besides the sense of failure that goes with this difficulty, the person is unable to readily keep appointments and can either become paranoid about them or dismiss them altogether. Our courts of law have to deal with this on a daily basis, with 'no show' being a constant problem.

It seems that we often attempt to teach children to use a clock, and to learn concepts of the time of day, without anchoring it to any useful pictorial notion — any bigger picture. As a result, they may learn that it is 2.35 but have no notion of what this really means in terms of the passing of the day.

To teach time, we need first to teach the bigger concept of what time looks like. It is useful to first create a picture of the day which encompasses the child's point of view and the child's experience. This can be seen to have a particular form and in a generalized style is presented in the diagram below.

The pictorial day

This visual depiction of the day is presented sequentially to the child, one bit at a time. We first draw the inner picture, which depicts a school day — from dawn on the left, through the sections of classroom and playground activity, to eventual nightfall on the right.

Having literally created a stylized picture of the child's day, we can then add numerals along our 'time-line', which coincide with the auditory or experiential information that we commonly present to children. e.g. '…at three o'clock, when the bell goes'.

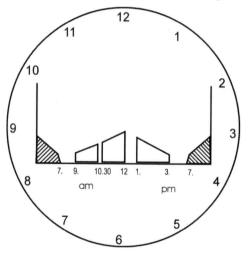

When presenting the child with this sequence of information, it is very important to ensure that they have fully grasped each preceding concept before presenting the next.

When the child has grasped the significance of this overlaying of information (the shape and the serial hour-times of the day) we can then move on and finally draw in the face of a clock (analogue) as an overlay to the pictorial concept of the day. This allows the child to start to identify where the significant points of the day lie on the face of the clock. Only after this has been satisfactorily achieved do we start to introduce the hands of the clock and learn what they indicate. With this carefully sequenced procedure, time will finally make useful sense to the child.

Annual concepts of time, such as the months, the seasons and the school holidays can be taught using a similar pictorial representation as per the illustration below.

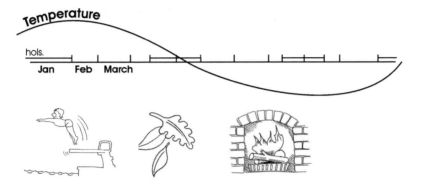

Other issues of time

The 'diesel/dyslexic' person is often completely unable to make any calculation in terms of the *passage of time* and is generally unable at any point to tell how far a day has progressed. Hence the school day and every academic exercise is like a never-ending dark tunnel without a predictable point of release.

With no sense of time, and no sense of the passage of time, they generally have no sense of other people's notion of *urgency*. Most parents and teachers have discovered that urging them to 'Hurry up' will be a waste of breath — and a waste of time. Being highly kinaesthetic, though, as well as specifically pictorial, the suggestion 'run' will usually bring heartening results.

Speed of speech can also be problematic for them, especially when it is a dynamic of instructional language. The pace of the parent's speech is really measured by the spaces between the words and the gaps between the sentences. These gaps are the spaces where the dyslexic listener examines, and brings sense to, the pictures created by the words they hear — or as is often the case, where they make futile attempts to put pictorial sense to the parent's non-pictorial language.

Without pauses which would allow them to process, the 'diesel/dyslexic' student is likely to struggle to follow the instruction, to fall further and further behind, and finally give up in confusion and disgust, believing themselves to be simply dumb and stupid. Unfortunately, teachers and parents who are not dyslexic themselves fail to understand what is happening and blame the child for not paying attention and for not listening. Disengagement creeps in.

Few concepts of time are pictorial, with the result that dyslexic children commonly suffer the indignity of not understanding concepts of time — including *sequence*, and that 'taking turns' is part of a sequence.

Do we naturally overcome these difficulties as we get older and become more exposed to the pressures of society? A consideration of the number of adults who are persistently late, who are paranoid about being late, or who find time pressure as being one of the major stressors of their life would suggest not.

Consistency, predictability and emotional security

Consistency
The human brain enjoys, and therefore seeks, *pattern*. Pattern is an essential element of *consistency* and is the part of our life that allows

us to deal with events in a knowing way. This *predictability* allows us to deal with moment-to-moment life in a way of *understanding* that minimizes the need for specific effort. We have all experienced the distress and exhaustion of protracted unpredictability in our personal lives.

In complex tasks such as learning to drive a car or mastering a foreign language, we seek the internal patterns (rules) which guide our behaviour and serve to make the complex easy. Music relies largely on pattern, and our mathematical systems allow us to cope with repeated occurrence through recognition of applied pattern.

Our notions of 'time' are a structural system applied within an observable pattern (solar/lunar cycles) that allow us to pattern events against divisions and subdivisions as small as one second and bigger than one year. We wake according to these patterns, we work according to these patterns, we start and we stop, we work and we play in a consistent and predictable manner according to these patterns — it may have nothing to do with reality, but it works. 'Time' is one of the significant (artificial) constructs that allows an individual and a society to recognize and use *pattern* to create *consistency* and *predictability* in day-to-day life. Without this we may lose our emotional security, become disorientated and anxious, destabilized and random in our actions, exhausted and in danger of spitting the dummy, earning ourselves unwanted labels!

Remember: the dyslexic child can't *see* time. Time is a fabrication of our human *imagination* but contrary to popular belief it has no *pictorial image* (yes, a contradiction of terms). This basic tenet of dyslexia is one we must always keep in mind: *if they cannot **see** it as a pictorial function, they are less able to **comprehend** it — and if they cannot comprehend it, they cannot do it.*

Although each individual child experiences this to a differing degree, as a parent, it is important to consider that your 'diesel/

dyslexic' child may have no comprehension of time — no comprehension of *your* time, no comprehension of your *concerns* about time or of how your *life revolves* around this nebulous notion. They surely know that other people get very upset about this but they cannot see it, cannot share it and cannot comprehend what it is or how it works. Nor, for that matter, why you get so uptight about it.

More than this, however, the child becomes super-aware that they have a deficit in this regard, that they are different, and that they have (yet another) area of shortfall. This leaves them feeling confused, inadequate and even guilty, and so they move to strategically correct their shortfall as best they are able. In this they are likely to rely heavily on *observable sequence*.

Not being able to register notions of time, the child uses their eyes to observe and establish sequences of behaviour or actions that make up their day. They quickly latch on to repetitive pattern, learning that in most situations one particular action will be predictably followed by another particular action. There may or may not be any specific relationship between the actions, but when they consistently occur in sequence, this sequence may become significant, and even pivotal for the child, impacting positively on their emotional security.

Hence, by way of example, where the family dog is consistently fed by the father before he comes to the dinner table at night (it stops the dog begging for scraps off the table), the child notes and learns this sequential relationship, and it becomes one of the structures of the passing of their day. However, when the grandparents are babysitting and inadvertently use a different routine ('Dogs get fed *after* dinner at our place'), the child's structural system is shaken, and their pattern is disestablished. To them this is like an unexpected obstacle on a well-known road, causing their emotional car to 'spin out'. In their confusion they may be unable to get back on track and so be unable to cope emotionally for the rest of the day.

This 'emotional spin-out' may occur when the class teacher is absent and a reliever comes for the day. It may happen when special events occur (e.g. a midweek evening social activity), or when an incident disrupts the predictable course of events — a flat tyre on the car. The child's reaction may seem to be out of all proportion to the significance of the event in our eyes, but we commonly don't realize just how central such small disruptions (to the child's sense of predictability) can be to the child who has no useful sense of time.

Predictability

For this reason, *predictability* should be fostered in the child's activities. For the child, benefit is gained from establishing a routine of activities that occur between 'get-up' time and departure for school, and for the events from dinnertime to bedtime. It is helpful to confirm these sequences through a series of drawings (much like a cartoon-strip) on the fridge or bedroom door and assist the child to use these as visual cues to a 'passage of process'.

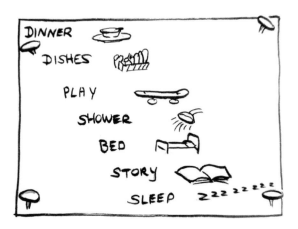

Similarly, family rituals play an important role in the life of any small child, like having an established seating position at the dinner table; a particular set bedtime and bedtime process; a known, set list of responsibilities around the house; and set schedules and systems for pocket money.

The child may not appear to take much notice of the list or drawings, but their presence will help them develop a system and pattern in their day.

Unexpected change

If it is the case that you suddenly need to deviate from or change the sequence of events, prepare the child verbally ahead of time, using positive statements that create a useful series of pictures for them:

'Josh, we normally go left out the gate, and drive straight to your school in the mornings. When we get in the car today, we have to go the other way to pick up Caroline. So, we will turn right out the gate, down the hill to Caroline's place, pick her up, then go through the middle of town to school. It is okay, and I will get you to school on time.'

Parenting style

The same principle applies to the style of the parents. If a parent is predictable in their response to certain activities or behaviours, the child will see the consistency and know where they stand. If the parent is inconsistent and unpredictable in their reactions, this confuses the child, who is then likely to test the moment and to test the boundaries looking for reliable guidelines.

Inconsistent and unpredictable parenting will therefore result in the child becoming unpredictable, erratic and conflictual. Here, rather than seeking to change and control the child's behaviour, we really need to change the parents' behaviour, so as to allow the child to settle.

In exactly the same way, consistency *between* the parents (where Mum's and Dad's style and reactions are similar) will help the child establish a consistent style themselves and they are less likely to play one parent against the other, and more likely to become a stable and sociable person.

Remember that

consistency

gives

predictability

gives

order and control

gives

emotional security

— and this helps make a happier child with a positive self-concept.

This is a significant positive factor in the life of the 'diesel/dyslexic' child, and the survival of the family as a unit.

Empowerment and disempowerment

For the typical 'diesel' child, there is huge danger that the dynamics of life will collude in such a way as to leave the child feeling powerless. The child who screams, hits out, disrupts and disembowels your family is telling you loud and clear about their frustration and their feeling of being disempowered. Although the child may not appear to you to be in any way disempowered, it is useful for you as a parent to see the behaviour that the child presents as being their compensation, their desperate reaction to their sense of being disempowered. As with most people, the behaviour that children present on the surface is more likely to represent what they feel they lack, rather than what they are. We may never understand it, but children do not act in this manner 'for no reason at all'.

The issue of whether or not the child is really disempowered is not the point. The real point is what the child feels — because, like anybody else, this is what they will react to.

Before looking at appropriate means to actively empower the child, let's take a moment to examine the personal and social role of *disempowerment*.

We consider ourselves to be 'human beings'. 'Being' is an active state — the active state of being human. We even recognize this in traditional greetings, such as 'How do you do?' 'Do' suggests activity and our implicit interest in what and how people do as being a measure of their place and state in society. But by definition the 'disempowered' person is a person of lesser 'do' ability.

If we take an otherwise capable person and restrict their capacity to 'do' in society by disempowering them in some way, it stands to reason that they will resent and resist this. Still motivated to participate, but stymied as to legitimate means to do so, some may doggedly hang on in and become the 'terriers' of society, protesting any and every social issue that reflects their disempowerment. Some, however, become compliant, dependent and even depressed, effectively accepting their depowered state, while others move to actively take back their power 'by fair means or foul'.

Empowering the child

If this is the case, and your child is in danger of feeling disempowered, what can we do about it?

We often approach young adults with the question *'What work are you going to do? What job are you wanting?'*, focusing them on a basal employment-related vision of participation. We are less inclined to focus on a qualitative view (*'How are you going to do it?'*), and we are even less inclined to direct their attention to the bigger, more philanthropic notions of *'Where do you fit in, and what could you contribute to society?'* There is little doubt that the world would be in a better state if more people considered what they could contribute to society, rather than what can they get out of it. Arguably the *'What is in it for me, how can I maximize my personal benefit?'* mentality has led to the current international social and fiscal meltdown.

'Empowerment' involves having the ability, the right, the opportunity and the wherewithal to achieve something. Having a *role* — even a set role — can give a basic sense of empowerment. However, if we introduce the notion of *options*, or of *choices*, this element of free will actively raises and personalizes the individual sense of empowerment. If we then add a sense of *voluntary load* or of 'responsibility', we are then moving to a notion of *inclusive empowerment* and to the betterment of our social environment.

Giving children roles and responsibilities in the running of the family home (e.g. feeding the family pet or ensuring that that all electrical plugs are disconnected before going on family holiday) is just one relatively simple and straightforward way to promote their sense of empowerment as a member of that group. However, over and above a sense of empowerment is a sense of place and inclusion readily facilitated by the setting of a clear raft of tasks and responsibilities in the home that are completely independent of the notion of payment.

In a home setting this could be facilitated by the family group 'think-tanking' a full list of regular tasks and responsibilities around the home, then asking for 'buy-in' from the various family members.

But what about their sense of empowerment as an individual, as a being in and of themselves?

Arguably, in our society the most obvious source of individual empowerment is via money. (Money: a symbolic measurement of our time, energy or intellectual input — a unit of exchange for material resources or reciprocal favours.)

One of the simple and appropriate ways we can empower a child is to give them access to money. Giving them *access* to money, though, is different from simply giving them money. The person who knows they can create money when they need or want to is a person who (in our society) has a certain level of personal empowerment.

The simple message here is: as one means of countering a feeling of personal disempowerment, rather than giving your child pocket money, *give them the means to earn pocket money in legitimate, accessible, predictable and reasonable ways.*

For example:

'Any time you need cash to go to the movies, you could wash the car, clean a few windows, mow the lawn or weed the veggie garden. The car is worth $4, one bucket of weeds $3, the lawn $5, and each panel of windows $1. You choose, do the work, and I'll pay.'

This is but one example of a simple and direct way to help a child find some sense of self-empowerment in their home context, and at the same time reinforcing the basic life philosophy of *'The more I am prepared to put in, the more I will be able to get out.'*

For more detailed information regarding parenting technique, the reader is referred to *With, Not Against* (King 2008).

Although all these issues addressed in this chapter are central to the child's survival in the home, they also apply equally to their survival and achievement at school.

> **For the dyslexic child, the accumulated persistent confusion and lack of success at both home and school, leads to frustration, anxiety, anger and depression.**

Chapter Ten
Classroom issues

The biggest impact of the 'diesel/dyslexic' style is seen in the classroom. In this chapter, we look again at how the child will present and how our established system is likely to work against them, with some comment on the price that the child, and the community, will pay as the child gets older.

- Indicators of pictorial thinking
- Which helping programme shall I use?
- Disengagement
- Teaching truths
- Responses to avoid
- Teacher style in the classroom
- Learning style

So, who is this child in your class, and how do we identify them?

Acknowledging the enormous professional workload carried by every classroom teacher, it is appropriate that we make answering this question a realistic exercise.

The risk in testing for dyslexia and in attempting to identify the specific child in the class is not that the wrong child may be included, but that this child may be excluded, and dismissed, on some other basis. The 'diesel' or dyslexic child may or may not be evident as such, and it is very easy to dismiss this child as just having 'an attitude problem', and just being a 'naughty child' or a child who is capable but disinterested and lazy.

When working/workshopping with teams of teachers, I ask them to take pencil and paper and jot down the name of any child in their class that comes to mind when I read out the following descriptors.

- The child in your class who demands a disproportionate amount of your energy.
- The child who may present a 'hard to like' personal style — the bully, the cheat, the liar, the surly one.
- The child who is disobedient and has an overt behaviour problem.
- The child who is a loner and perhaps a 'motor-mouth'.
- The child who is a compulsive fiddler, and 'fix-it' or 'break-it' person.
- The child who is uncoordinated, has left/right difficulties, cannot sit still, prints in capital letters, has repeated reversals, has spidery print, cannot start print close to the margin, persistently rubs out or starts a new page.
- Any left-handed child.

Every classroom teacher is likely to have up to five names on their list at this stage, all of whom are likely to fit as 'diesels' in one way or another. They may or may not fit the teacher's perception of dyslexic (and should not be labelled as such) and there may yet be other children in the class who should also be on that list.

This is simply one place to start.

Indicators of pictorial thinking

A full list of characteristics that are often seen in dyslexic children is included earlier in this book (Chapter Three), and parents or teachers could use them to scope the broader parameters of the dyslexic style.

However, beyond this the list below is included as part of our process of 'narrowing the field'. They are included as potential indicators of what a teacher may see in a 'pictorial thinker' who is experiencing frustration in the learning environment.

Dyslexia and a 'pictorial thinking style' should be considered when a child presents in the following way:

- Academic achievement is lower than what the teacher's knowledge of that child would lead them to expect.
- Behaviour and attitude to classwork reflect significant frustration and anxiety — and even anger.
- Gives evidence of being confused about directionality.
- Presents with a speech impediment or has indistinct speech.
- The child (or their parent) prints using a combination of upper- and lower-case letters.
- Demonstrates foot or eye preference inconsistent with their hand preference.
- Prints with reversed letters or reversed sequence after seven years of age.
- Printing shows that they prescribe letters other than in the 'correct' manner.
- Shows evidence of using rote memory as a prime reading tool.
- Shows a real disinclination to read or write.
- Uses a fresh page after any error of print or imperfect achievement.

- Persistently starts out from the margin.
- Has difficulty following or is slow to comply with instruction.
- Forgets what they have been told to do.
- Does what they have been specifically told *not* to do.
- Shows confusion regarding sequence, concepts of time or days of the week.
- Does not handle unexpected change or change from routine.
- Persistently forgets what they were going to say.
- Cannot remember names of things or people.
- Has a very fragile self-concept.
- Gives evidence of being hyperactive or has a very short attention span in class.
- Has accumulated previous school reports with comments typical of those listed earlier in Chapter Three ('Common descriptors', page 73).

Yes, it is the case that this list could include many of the children in any classroom — and maybe this is the point. The pictorial thinking style (and its difficulties) is a lot more prevalent than is generally recognized, and rather than being seen as an aberrant style, and the domain of learning difficulties, it needs to be accepted as a legitimate element of the thinking of most mainstream people — and the predominant style of those who may be dyslexic.

In all probability, the pictorial thinking mode — which is arguably broader, faster and more creative than the linguistic form — has been the predominant thinking mode since prehistory, and as such has been the prime source of technological evolution in the world. The wheel, the steam engine, the internal combustion engine, the aeroplane, the lever, the cantilever bridge — the basic building blocks of society as we know it — were probably all created and developed within the image-based minds of pictorial thinkers.

It is only in relatively recent years that modern-day theoretical education systems, based on linguistic processes, have assumed their prevalent role. Our education system has become skewed towards linguistic thinking and has created the 'problem' that it has called dyslexia.

In this we have bypassed the inclusion of pictorial skills as part of our formal classroom process, and robbed the predominantly pictorial thinkers of learning, of skills, of qualifications and legitimacy.

In fairness to these children, the mindset that regards some children as 'naughty, unmotivated and lazy or dull' must be relinquished and transcended. Rather than having these children actively marginalized, or in some cases professionally tested, labelled then allocated specialist funds or skills, they — and their style — need to be legitimized as being normal, valid and valued.

The more we focus on labelling, on defining, on testing and on establishing programmes for dyslexic children, the more we are effectively blaming the victim.

In doing this we actively distract the focus from an educational and teaching style that marginalizes a significant section of our community.

When we accept the evidence that it is our educational style that creates dyslexia, we can then put our energy into broadening our system to include and normalize the pictorial thinking mode.

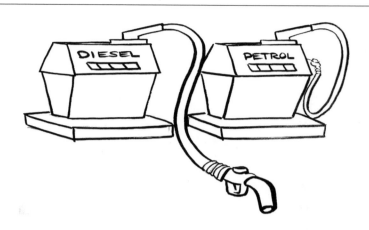

Now, having gained some knowledge of the possible range of personal behaviours and characteristics of the dyslexic child, with just a passing acquaintance with some of their personal sensitivities and idiosyncrasies, we will take a closer look at how it all so frequently comes unstuck within the walls of the classroom — despite the best efforts of our skilled and dedicated teachers.

But first we will deal with a question that is embedded in parental desperation.

Which helping programme shall I use?

Having presented over 500 training seminars to parents and teachers in New Zealand and Australia, I receive a continuous stream of feedback from parents bemoaning what they see as the insensitivity of some teachers in relation to their child's perceived needs. Although they often have no clear idea how it may be achieved, these parents want a better deal for their kids. Many of them end up looking outside the school system, to individual coaching or to private programmes, for their answer.

One of the subsequent questions I am asked relates to the effectiveness of a range of potential 'booster' educational programmes for the dyslexic child. As anybody who has attempted to open this can of worms will know, there are many approaches and programmes being offered, from basically free, to as much as $9000 per child, and with many claiming wonderful outcomes, most of which I would cynically suggest could be achieved as the simple by-product of a structured one-to-one programme, and all the attention and energy input that that entails.

My simple response to these enquiries is that in reality it is not so much the programme that matters but the personality and style of the teacher. As anybody in the industry will tell you, a 'teacher' can destroy any programme — and any child for that matter — through old-fashioned insensitivity. It is not the programme that is really the issue but rather the personal style and the approach used by the person implementing the programme. A positive, sensitive and supportive friend can help the fragile student achieve those critically important basic learning blocks that are so essential to successful academic achievement.

Disengagement

When I ask adult 'dyslexics' about their schooling years, and specifically ask what it was that made the positive difference in that nightmare setting, the response I get is something along the lines of, 'Miss Jones. She made the difference.'

And further questioning suggests that what the Miss Joneses of the world did that was so significant can be adequately summed up as *'Gave time, consideration and TLC'*.

So there you go: as far as the 'dyslexics' of the world are

concerned, what any teacher needs to do, in order to deal with the problems associated with this elusive, amorphous thing called dyslexia, is give copious quantities of time, consideration and tender loving care!

Great — but not great, as any teacher would just roll their eyes and sigh, asserting that this is exactly what they have been doing their entire teaching career, and the situation still seems to be getting worse. So, rather than giving up at this point, let's look at the scene from a different angle to see if we can find some better sense, or at least a way in.

If we were to focus on the negative classroom experience of both the student and the teacher, we could say that it is characterized by an overriding notion of *disengagement* — meaning that the child has effectively withdrawn their energy and is to some extent removed from what is going on in the lesson.

This could include:

- being bored and dreamy in class and not paying full attention
- being physically present, but otherwise withdrawing their energy from the situation (except perhaps to entertain themselves)
- being physically absent from class
- leaving school and any further training as soon as they reach the age that the law allows them to do so.

Although it could be argued that 'being physically absent from class' is really only an issue at secondary level, its preliminary forms are well documented at primary level and are evident in most if not all schools.

If it is the case that active disengagement is at least one of the major factors in the educational career of the dyslexic child, it certainly behoves us to ask what measures we can possibly take to prevent this creeping disease. In fact, this is a commonly asked question and is being examined by skilled educators all over the world.

Unfortunately, when we ask a question of this nature, we typically lead ourselves into looking for gaps in our system, for things that we could add to our teaching repertoire, do instead of, differently or better. What we are less inclined to do is examine our current belief systems, our current understandings of 'good practice', or even 'best practice', and check to see if they really are effective and worthwhile as we believe.

Working one to one for many years with both children and adults who have experienced difficulty in our education system, I have enjoyed a privileged position and a privileged relationship, and via this have been given information that, sadly, has taken me a lifetime to process and understand. Although I seldom have directly asked ten-year-old children what it is that teachers do that makes the classroom situation so intolerable for them, when I look back and sense their frustration, anxiety and anger, I recognize a common theme in the feedback they have been giving me. For them it is not about what the teachers are not doing that creates their difficulties, but rather it is about what the teachers need to *stop doing*.

Their feedback strongly suggests that teachers as a body hold, value and are guided by a whole range of beliefs and practices ('truths') basic to accepted teaching philosophy and style that incrementally erode the dyslexic students' self-concept, their experience of success, their willingness to participate, and their active engagement in the classroom.

The feedback from the children themselves is that their failure and withdrawal is a response to teacher belief and teaching style, and that teachers are unwittingly undermining the achievement of some children in the classroom, inadvertently creating the very problem that they are working so hard to remove.

Although such a statement will predictably and understandably generate an indignant self-protective response from the teaching profession, there may be more value in it than some are initially willing to allow.

Yes, it is the case that exhaustive and ongoing research has led us to our classroom philosophies, beliefs and style, and that the overwhelming evidence is that this has led to some remarkable and positive techniques and approaches in teaching. However, despite this, we know that it is still the case that our system does not work for a significant proportion of the children. Ironically but understandably, these are the children who consume a disproportionate amount of any individual teacher's energy and patience.

The paragraphs below focus on 'teaching truths' — beliefs that are so implicit to our teaching headspace that often we do not even recognize that we hold them or comply with them in our teaching practice.

These 'teaching truths' have evolved because they equate with effective teaching with most of the children in the classroom, and we naturally hold fast to methods that are seen to be effective. But we know they are only effective for *most* of the children we teach. What we fail to see is that for other children these very same principles, methods and strategies may be actively problematic.

The list below includes common teacher beliefs, stance or speech, each of which, in the author's belief, will impact negatively on the 'learning difficulty' child. The list may appear extensive, but it is certainly not complete. As each of the points cited has been dealt with specifically in other parts of this book, the explanatory comments here on each have been specifically minimized.

Teaching truths

As we grow and mature in life, we progressively accumulate elements of philosophy and belief that become our 'truths' — a set of guiding principles that unconsciously direct us through the interfaces of our day-to-day life. Similarly, experienced teachers unconsciously accumulate knowledge and beliefs that govern their interactions with children in the classroom. As valid and useful as these may be with most of the pupils in a classroom, they may be destructive to the self-esteem and learning ability of our dyslexic student. Although appearing to be good practice, the following 'teaching-truths' will predictably work against those students.

1. The teacher's use of the words *'just'*, *'try'* and *'it's easy'* helps simplify issues and encourages children's effort.
   (But when the child is finding it difficult, these words just emphasize that they are overtly stupid.)
2. 'Motivation' is a singular dynamic for the teacher to address with each student.
   (Motivation is an internal dynamic and differs for every child. A teacher cannot motivate a child but can manipulate outcomes that the child may — or may not — find motivating.)
3. Teacher praise will help raise a child's self-concept and encourage effort.
   (Like motivation, self-concept is internal to the child and, when low, is seldom raised by external dynamics like praise. It can be raised by positive experience but is easily shattered by negative comment. Overt praise from a teacher is more likely to cause a child with low self-concept to withdraw effort for fear of disillusioning the teacher. Affirmation may be more effective.)

4. 'Feedback' equates with 'motivation'.

   (*A child fearful of failure or rejection will focus on any potentially negative aspect of the feedback and is likely to respond negatively.*)

5. Children who will not participate are not motivated.

   (*The child who is disengaged, or used to failing, may be strongly motivated to withdraw effort in order to avoid further failure. Their motivation is to self-protect.*)

6. Teacher-led questioning helps stimulate student thinking.

   (*True for some, but for others the abstract nature of much questioning — who, why, where, what, how — will be too confusing and cause them to disengage. 'I wonder what … I wonder where … I wonder how …' might be more productive.*)

7. It is natural and normal for children to be able to formulate and ask questions as an information-seeking process.

   (*Yes, except for dyslexic children, who will look for visual rather than linguistic cues.*)

8. It is natural and normal that children engage in 'self-talk' (inner dialogue) as a way of processing information.

   (*Inner dialogue is so central and natural for most of us that we find it difficult to comprehend that to varying degrees dyslexic children are unable to use this thinking tool.*)

9. Maths and number concepts can be appropriately presented via written or oral language, and as such they are a test of advanced comprehension. See Chapter 11.

   (*Presenting the mechanics of maths as a linguistic exercise can put it beyond the scope and comprehension of the dyslexic student.*)

10. Spoken and written words adequately connote specific meaning.

    (Many English words have colloquial origins markedly different from their current common usage. Lyft *is an old English word for* left, *meaning* wrong.)

11. Language is the principal and appropriate teaching, learning and assessment device for schools.

    (Unless of course the student is dyslexic, finds language inherently confusing, and would learn better, and demonstrate their learnings better, through other modalities.)

12. A deficit in language skill generally equates with a deficit in 'intelligence'.

    (Although few teachers would overtly agree with this statement, their actual behaviour would often tell a different story.)

13. 'Certification' equates with accomplishment and with learned skill.

    ('Certification' in academic areas is largely dependent on speed of handwriting and extent of personal vocabulary, mixed with linguistic memory. Information written about a topic certainly does not equate to skill within the topic.)

14. 'How', 'Which', 'Why', 'What', 'When' are useful entry points for creative thinking.

    (As mentioned above, these cues are too abstract (non-visual) to be useful notions for the dyslexic brain.)

15. Verbal expression in response to specific questioning is an appropriate mechanism to assess a child's knowledge.

    (For the dyslexic child, questioning equates with interrogation and raises confusion, anxiety and fear of failure — which sabotage their ability to perform.)

16. Listening to a child reading aloud is an appropriate way to test the child's reading ability.

    (Reading aloud is many times more complex and more difficult than reading silently. Asking a child to read aloud can be a very effective way to destroy any interest or pleasure in reading they may have.)

17. Silence is an integral part of the writing process.

    (Lacking skills in 'self-talk', the dyslexic child may benefit from being able to scope their story through oral interaction with another child or teacher aide. See Ernest in Chapter One.)

18. The left-to-right orientation/process of the Arabic reading/ writing system is a natural and appropriate system for all learners.

    (Few people ever stop to question the left-to-right process of our written language, to discover that it is a function of our right-handed predominance, and that left-handers have a natural tendency to move right to left across the page. They thus fail to ever appreciate that left-handers, and most 'dyslexics', are required by our 'system' to do all reading and writing activities in a manner that is back to front for them — irrespective of which hand they write with. See Chapter Eleven.)

19. It is appropriate and necessary for teachers to continuously assess the performance of children — but not for children to assess or criticize the performance of the teacher.

    (Although we are comfortable constantly assessing and rating children and their performance, we deny younger beings the right to have any valid opinion of those adults who are instrumental in their educational development.

Why do we deny children any useful mechanisms to give constructive feedback to their teachers? What is the fear?)

20. 'Behaviour problems' are the product of 'attitude problems' or of personal emotional difficulties.
    (Anxiety, frustration, confusion and anger associated with the centrality of language to our educational process create the behavioural difficulties we are so often confronted with in school children.)

21. Drawing a child's attention to their errant behaviour will help them take control of it.
    (This may be true of children with a positive self-concept, but not so with the children we are concerned with here, whose levels of self-esteem may be very low.)

22. 'Punishment' equates with 'discipline' and helps children develop self-control.
    (Perhaps true for some. For others who feel misjudged, punishment will only cause resentment, alienation and a consolidation of negativity.)

23. 'Loss of privilege' is a useful and appropriate control strategy in the classroom.
    (The resultant student humiliation, anger and resentment will never create a conducive learning environment.)

24. 'Don't' implies the opposite of 'Do'.
    (The verbal command 'Don't run' has only one visual component — 'run'. This visual component of the command has more impact on the dyslexic child than the abstract and contradictory linguistic notion of 'do not'.)

25. Children often have 'selective' hearing.
    (Dyslexic children will 'hear' words that register a pictorial message, but not words that convey no visual imagery at

all. Therefore, they will hear and visualize the words such as 'jet fighter', but not the word 'respect'.)

26. Children can control what they 'pay attention' to and what they don't 'pay attention' to.

    (A speaker who utilizes humour, specifically pictorial language or visual cues, will be more likely to retain the child's attention over a speaker whose language is more abstract.)

27. 'Time' is a meaningful concept to children.

    (Unless the concept of time is presented and taught with specifically visual links, it will remain a confusing concept for many. See Chapter Nine.)

28. Dyslexia is a learning difficulty.

    (Dyslexic children have a specific style of learning. Until a teacher becomes familiar with this style it can create a teaching difficulty.)

29. 'ADD' children have an attention deficit disorder.

    (Children labelled as ADD generally have less ability to screen out unwanted or insignificant environmental stimuli. They therefore tend to be bombarded by sensory input at all levels, and in truth are exhausted by their AOD — attention overload difficulty. See Chapter Six.).

Every point included in this list is discussed as a potential stumbling block to classroom achievement of dyslexic children in other chapters of this book.

Responses to avoid

Now we continue with the theme of 'misunderstandings causing miscommunications', and how despite our best intentions we can, as teachers, sabotage our own objectives. Without wishing to labour the notion that we as parents or teachers may inadvertently be part of the problem, it is important that we be very clear as to when and how this could be the case.

Interpreting, misinterpreting or understanding the child's style

Intuition, training and experience all come together and guide teachers and parents in perceiving, understanding and responding to children's behaviour. Through these we learn what is acceptable and what is not acceptable, what is useful and what is distracting in our learning environment, and consequently we develop a mental list of observed behaviours that we deem to be unacceptable, and that we therefore choose to address in children.

This is normal human behaviour and to be expected of any parent or classroom teacher. But what if our understanding, and therefore our response, is based on a misinterpretation, on a misunderstanding of what is really going on for the child?

In the following pages we examine some of the less-acceptable behaviours commonly seen in children, and suggest that, especially in the case of 'diesels', both the adult and the child may benefit from a bigger understanding of what is going on. The difficulties associated with the scenarios below are generally a product of:

- The child having difficulty with language — receiving it, thinking with it, speaking with it, writing it, reading it.

- The child being primarily a visual, pictorial person.
- The child being highly tactile, hands on and practical.

'Look at me when I am talking to you. I can tell when you are not listening.'

The 'diesel' child is primarily visual. The teacher is talking, asking the child to listen — which is fair enough, but listening is not their strength area. If they are looking at the teacher their energy is going to their eyes, not their ears. So, to focus on their hearing they turn their eyes away, divert them, allowing the energy to go to their ears so that they can hear, listen and hopefully understand.

'Put that down, stop fiddling, and listen.'

The 'diesel' child is tactile, kinaesthetic and hands on. When we pick up an object, sensors in our fingertips relay a message to the brain that we are ready for action — fingertip touch switches the brain on. What we are seeing with these children is that, in order to cope with the difficult classroom situation, they are fiddling, stimulating the fingertips, keeping their brains constantly stimulated. (Digging fingernails into your opposite fingertips is a great way to stay alert while driving too.)

Let them fiddle — with something that will stimulate brain activity.

'Sit still in your chair!'

Typically, these children find it harder to sit still than to move, so they will burn up more energy trying but failing to sit still and be more distracted trying to comply than if you just let them be. Ironically, asking them to do certain leg exercises or arm stretching after they have written a word, or at the end of each page read, will legitimize their need, as well as help them relax — or at least burn off some of that excess energy.

'Don't touch. You don't look with your hands.'

The truth is just the opposite — these children do look with their hands, and they actually cannot really 'get to grips' with something unless they can touch it. They do need to be 'in touch'.

'Engage brain before opening mouth.'

Unfortunately, this is one of the ultimate put-downs for the 'diesel' person. They do not have the ability to assess what words they will use before they say them. They come out of their mouth, and they hear them at that stage — and often wish that they had never said them.

They don't understand how other people can do it, so just assume that they are dumb and stupid. The only control they have is to refrain from speaking at all. Some manage this and go silent, becoming socially withdrawn. However, spontaneity is part and parcel of the 'diesel' style, and even in my seventies I still manage to regularly put my foot in it!

'Don't put your hand up unless you know the answer.'

The child hears your language and their brain responds in its visual thinking mode. They see the movie or picture in their head, eagerly put their hand up, then struggle to find words that equate with the pictures, often contributing a great meandering discourse of verbiage which was not what the teacher really wanted.

But, further, it may be a *movie* that the child is seeing in their head, and after about three seconds the image that applied to your question has gone and the movie has moved on — but the child's hand is still up. Hence when the teacher finally asks for the child's input, their comment is an embarrassed *'Ah, I forget'*. After a while, they learn not to try — or at least not to participate.

'I know you know it — you knew it yesterday.'

The first issue of difficulty here is that although there is generally not a difficulty with memory — 'diesels' can remember anything they have seen or can get a picture of — there often is a problem in locating that specific memory.

Crudely speaking, we store and memorize information in a pigeonhole system where the information byte is registered via a labelling system. The problem for the 'diesel' is that they are paying attention to so many visual things at once (not ADD, but rather AOD — attention *overload* difficulty) that they have no idea what label the memory is pigeonholed under. They simply can't find where the memory is stored.

The school caretaker's mower may have been going past the window when the child last pulled that memory out ('The longest river in New Zealand is the Waikato'), but that information is then put back into storage under 'Tractor/lawnmower/clover smell'.

The other factor here is straight out, old-fashioned *fear*. Fear of *rejection* causes fear of *'not being good enough'*. This feeds the fear of *failure*, which in turn creates the fear of *attempting*. An instantaneous fear response floods the child and their brain does a 'white-out' — just like we experience on the ski slopes. In this state they have no access to memory, or to language, or to any useful response. We see this in children, we see it commonly in men in emotionally challenging situations, and it still happens to the author on a painfully regular basis.

'Well, it can't have been important.'

This is very similar to the point above. The child has seen something really exciting and wants to share it with you, the most important adult in their life at that moment. They rush inside with a head full of movie and their brain firing off in its normal visual thinking mode. But when they find you, you are on the phone or in the middle of another conversation, and so you have to wait a few seconds before you can give them the attention they demand.

But, remember, what they see in their head is a movie and the film keeps on running, and the scene in their mind's eye keeps changing. By the time you get back to them, five seconds have elapsed and the scene in their head has moved on and completely changed. They can't rerun it, can't reverse it, and so they have no recall of what it was that they wanted to share with you five seconds ago.

They are embarrassed, feel stupid and dumb, and have to say, 'Ah, I forget'.

'Start from the beginning — and speak slowly.'

The child rushes in, bursting with a flood of verbal approximations that make no sense to you at all. 'Hey, Miss, on the way to school, like, this car, and blood, but he wasn't hurt, and the man, fast, man, fast as, and CRAAAAASH! I saw it ...'

In your normal supportive way, you want to help with a little structure, and you say, 'Stop. Start at the beginning, speak slowly and tell me what happened.' Lovely, but that doesn't work for the child.

Remember, in their head are movies — and in this case possibly at least three movie screens are replaying different aspects of what they saw, simultaneously.

When we ask the child to stop talking, the movies keep on running, and they lose the pertinent picture. They are already jumping from screen to screen trying to grab some pertinent words so as not to lose the essence before each movie moves on, and this is why they can't speak slowly; they don't have time! When we ask them to start at the beginning we lose them, because in their mind's eye there are a number of movies, so for them there is no specific beginning to start at.

'Don't repeat my question, just give me an answer.'
With the dyslexic person the process here is like a Google search on your laptop. You put the words on the screen, but nothing happens until you push the Enter key. The child is effectively not able to process your question until they have converted it to their visual mode, and they do this by repeating the question to themselves aloud — and usually moving their eyes up and to the side (as per neurolinguistic programming — NLP).

They are not stalling for time and nor are they being evasive. They are doing what they need to do to give you what you want.

'You did hear, you do remember, you did understand' (Usually followed by 'This is deliberate disobedience.')
The bigger picture here runs: *'What did I just tell you?' 'You said no diving.' 'And what did you just do?' 'I dived.' 'So you did hear, you do remember, you did understand — this is deliberate disobedience...'*

This child is likely to end up labelled ODD (oppositional defiant disorder — which is seen as a need to defy authority and do exactly what they have been told not to do), or CPD (cognitive processing disorder), or sometimes even APD (auditory processing disorder), with the explanation given that they either don't hear *don't*, or that they think *don't* means *do*.

It is too easy to come up with explanations that simply blame the child, that suggest that there is something wrong with the child — which lets us off the hook, so we don't need to look at what we might need to do differently.

To really understand this, it is helpful to look back at the dual brain continuum.

In a nutshell, when we say, 'Think of a tennis racket', the listener will automatically get a picture of a tennis racket in their mind's eye. However, when we say 'Don't think of the Eiffel Tower', the listener will automatically get a picture of the Eiffel Tower — which they may then quickly replace with a French beret or something, anything, so as to get rid of that picture of the Eiffel Tower!

When we say, 'No diving', the listener, dyslexic or not, will get a picture of diving, and the non-dyslexic person will also get the non-pictorial message 'no'. The dyslexic will just get the picture and will then act on it (hypnosis) — and be as confused as us by their own behaviour. When asked to, they can remember and repeat back to us the actual words of the instruction ('you said no diving') and then it all turns to custard, with us concluding that either they are deliberately defiant or there is something wrong with the child.

'Why did you do that?'

The word 'why?' is not pictorial, and in this context it has little meaning for the child. (Yes, they may use it a lot themselves, but strangely that is a different issue.) Basically, there is no 'why' around their action, they just reacted, they did it, and any deep emotional causes underlying their actions are a complete mystery to them. They do not have a real answer to this question, and asking them 'why' just increases the guilt and the resentment.

'Are there any questions?' 'Do you understand?'

Basically, questions have got to involve language. To process information in such a manner as to formulate questions involves 'inner language' — sometimes known as 'inner dialogue' or 'self-talk'. The dyslexic person is thus unlikely to be able to formulate questions, let alone find the words to ask them.

Questioning as a teaching technique

This demands that we stop for a moment and consider one of the very basic tenets of the western teaching system. Our teachers are actively trained to put questions to students, in the belief that questions stimulate the thinking process and therefore stimulate the whole learning process.

And if we were all language operators ('petrol thinkers'), and if none of us were predominantly pictorial ('diesel thinkers'), this would probably be valid thinking. But it is not okay to orientate our teaching technique to favour some (yes, the majority) of the students, and to actively sideline others.

We explained above the debilitating impact that questions can have on the non-linguistic student, especially when the question focuses on non-pictorial information. However, with insight, teachers can reword questions so as to allow the pictorial student to access their pictorial brain and therefore be actively involved in the lesson.

For example, a linguistic question *'What do you think might be the purpose of a recycling station?'* could be reworded as:

'In the weekend I loaded the back of my car up with old bottles and an old lawn mower. I drove down to the Recycling Centre where the man told me where to put them. (See what has already happened in the reader's pictorial brain.) *I'm wondering*

what happens to them now, where they go to, and why we do this.'

Note that there is no actual question here at all — it is all a statement based on the assertion 'I am wondering...' — a brilliant way of getting other people to ponder the same issue, and therefore to stimulate involvement and the learning process.

'Is this your best work?'

Obviously, if the teacher has seen fit to ask this question, there is something less than satisfactory about the work the child has done. However, the nature of the question immediately puts the child into a no-win position. If they answer 'Yes' it will be an unacceptable answer, and equally, if they answer 'No' it will still be unacceptable. Simply put, there is no point in trapping the child like this as it will only cause resentment.

If you want the child to put more effort in, deliberately create a positive relationship with the child. They are then more likely to work to *please* you, rather than to annoy you.

'Don't shout out — put your hand up and wait your turn.'

The child stands to lose the relevant picture in their head if made to wait. Knowing that they have an answer right now and wanting to be an active participant in the classroom process, they really have no option other than to shout out immediately. Despite our traditional style, it might make good sense to actively encourage such behaviour in some learning contexts.

'Go and play with somebody — make some friends.' And 'We all have to learn to be team players.'

Although not always the case, it is very common that the 'diesel' child is a natural loner and they are happiest on their own. They think and work differently, take a different track to arrive at their destination, and may arrive at quite different thinking destinations from other children.

However, to require the child to work in groups may serve to severely cramp their style and actively limit their achievement. Similarly, to expect them to play with others, in either formal or informal activities, may be an unfair expectation. It is likely that they will not understand the overt, let alone the covert, rules of society.

In our schools there is often pressure for children to join team sports, whereas these children would often be more comfortable with individual sports such as chess or track events or motocross riding.

However, if it is insisted that the child joins the local team, let them be the fullback or the goalie — some position in 'the team' where in essence they play an individual game.

'Tell me how you are feeling' or 'What do you think about that?'

A fair enough question for a teacher or counsellor to ask — if the child has a reasonable linguistic capability. For the pictorial thinker, there may be no available response, other than the 'big-shoulder' response: a shrug and 'I dunno'.

Better that we use an 'I wonder…' statement here. *I'm wondering how you feel about that, whether it is comfortable or not. Maybe, when you're ready you could let me know.'*

'Just another imaginary sore tummy!'

All teachers have met the child who wants to avoid certain classroom activities, so invents aches and pains that require a sojourn in the sick bay. They make out that they are feeling sick — or do they?

In the author's own childhood experience the pains were real, and almost certainly the product of chronic anxiety, and he has lived his entire life with the results of those 'imaginary sore tummies' that rapidly grew into full-blown stomach ulcers. Having the pains was one thing but having them completely dismissed by the adults and authorities in life, and being blamed for all the associated difficulties, can leave a child with a huge distrust of authority people, and a distrust of their own sensitivities, with predictable outcomes for their later life.

'He is okay — he is just shy.'

The child who is shy is simply a person whose social behaviour is dominated by the fear of not being good enough, and so carries a major fear of failure. This might be the outcome of a lack of confidence, a lack of knowledge, a lack of skill, a lack of exposure — or of a history of a lack of success. This person generally does not respond well to pressure to perform but is more likely to respond to subtle and gentle support to attempt sequential approximations of the desired activity.

Many children (and adults) initially express this in the way they stand and in the way they articulate their words. Basic acting lessons in physical stance, hand position and use of voice can be a very productive place to assist.

So, yes when I talk to 'diesel/dyslexic' students about what teachers could do in the classroom to make things easier, the answer I get is so often about what teachers should *stop doing*.

Unfortunately, despite teachers being highly motivated, and utilising what they have learned to do under the banner of 'best practice', these mechanisms have the potential to be very disabling for the 'diesel' students.

Teacher style in the classroom

What can we do?

It is all very well describing the child and their characteristics, listing all their specific needs and even looking at how parent or teacher responses might inadvertently work against the child. The eventual question, however, will focus on that very difficult task of prescribing what we *can* do that is likely to be specifically useful to this child for their success in the classroom.

Remembering that every teacher is an expert in their own particular way, and that every teacher has their own unique style, we will refrain from attempting to teach Gran to suck eggs. Below is just a short list, guidelines, of style to use in the classroom. Nothing new, but potentially useful to the struggling student — dyslexic or not.

- As the child leaves the classroom each afternoon, a simple *'See you tomorrow'* or *'See you after the weekend'* helps remove a lot of the anxiety associated with their difficulty with knowing the days of the week — 'Is tomorrow another school day?'
- Indicate where we are up to in the day via a daily timeline across the top of the whiteboard. An indicator of where time is up to — a timeline, rather than the face of a clock.
- If you are a social worker and have an appointment with a dyslexic person, a simple phone text two hours beforehand can make all the difference. They might even turn up.
- Slow your rate of speech. Put bigger spaces between your sentences. Speak clearly and slowly, without running your words together.

- Use language that is pictorial and where the pictures convey the appropriate message. If necessary, restate something in a more pictorial way.
- Use demonstrations and stories and humour to emphasize the point.
- Use eye contact, and address students by name.
- Give constant positive feedback — for effort, for participation, for approximation — but using *affirmation* rather than praise.
- Avoid the use of non-pictorial terms whenever possible, e.g. 'purpose'.
- Recognize and allow for the students' need to move, to walk, to touch.
- Utilize humour in your presentation — but avoid sarcasm — and be prepared to 'act the clown'.
- Teach with the active participation of the students wherever possible.
- Encourage active debate, seek out the pros and cons, and deliberately seek alternative ways of viewing situations.
- Avoid asking direct questions as such. Start your process with 'I'm wondering...' as a good alternative to generate responses.
- Be specifically positive towards students who are struggling. This is particularly uplifting for them.

Learning style

As a final contribution to this chapter, where we have been focusing on the child and developing an understanding of their inner working, we look briefly at the interactions between the child and teacher (or parent) in terms of questions and answers, goal-setting and devising ways to assist the child to become an explorer and self-discovering thinker.

A lifetime of observing children in the classroom, focusing on the teaching/learning interactions between children and adults, indicates certain common processes and techniques that occur. Some are planned and deliberate; others are reactionary with unrecognized impact.

As with other points of focus, there is value in pausing to ask ourselves: 'Are we achieving what we think/plan/hope to achieve here?'

A few notes regarding teaching style, as it relates to children's natural learning style, may allow a re-evaluation of our own processes here.

Children's questions

Children will naturally ask both naive and searching questions. This arises from their ability to see and understand only to a certain level and their intrigue as to the connections they implicitly recognize but cannot see or identify.

Many parents and teachers see it as their duty and role to provide an answer to children's questions. This comes from our own need to feel that we are adequately fulfilling our responsibility in the parent or teacher role. After all, don't good questions deserve good answers? Maybe not.

When a child asks a question, they indicate an expanding mental state — a 'space' is happening in their thinking, indicating that an opportunity for specific learning is currently available. This is the space for 'teaching to the moment', and herein lies an opportunity ... and a danger. When a parent or teacher (with the best intention) responds in such a manner as to *answer* that question, the chances are that the child will accept that answer as being 'the answer'. Now they 'know', their need is fulfilled and so their thinking is likely to stop there.

An answer to a question supplies a unit of 'information' which is limited by the thinking capacity and experience of the adult. It may or may not be accurate or useful information, but it is not the child's own knowledge, as it is not the product of the child's own processing or experience. By answering children's questions, we are in danger of inadvertently limiting their thinking and their knowledge. We may even mislead them with our misunderstandings, and we may steal the development of their further thinking around that question.

An alternative response might be something like:

'That's a good question, and I'm wondering what you already know about that.'

Or *'How about you take that question home as homework tonight and see what we can come up with tomorrow?'*

Or *'Good one. Any suggestions of how we go about researching that?'*

Or *'Okay team, what information can we put on the table that may help us get a useful answer here?'*

Or *'The simple answer to that question might be ... But what happens if we dig a bit deeper into this?'*

Goal-orientated learning

Our current western educational process favours 'goal-orientated' learning. Although there are distinct benefits in this, we should also be aware of the potential downside.

While 'teaching goals', or 'learning goals', give us a track to go down, and structures to keep on that track, in many ways 'goals' are dangerously akin to 'answers' in that they create an artificial focus point, a target or an outcome, that in itself (once reached) can prematurely terminate the thinking or development process. (Goal reached, tick the box, change the topic.)

Of even greater concern, however, is the fact that once a goal has been chosen and set, the direction of the thinking that subsequently takes place is directed and constrained by that goal. At all points along the way the thinking/exploring process is persistently and unconsciously reset towards that goal, predicting the targeted outcome of the thinking and precluding alternative pathways.

In this way it is quite possible that our carefully chosen 'goals', 'answers' and 'definitions' all stand to lock and foreclose our thinking.

Expansive thinking

Questions both indicate and invite expansive thinking. 'Expansive thinking' can be facilitated by the 'thinking process' where the adult (teacher or parent) is able to use or teach the child to use a series of clarificatory steps that will help facilitate exploration of issues and subsequent learning.

Expansive thinking does not invite accumulation of 'facts' (which may act in a similar manner to 'answers' and close the thinking process) but rather of 'associations' that may invite a closer examination, lead to a greater understanding of the situation, and be in themselves a platform for further thinking beyond.

To facilitate such expansive thinking, it is recommended therefore that we move beyond the traditional type of stimulatory question (e.g. *'Why, do you think, do some clouds move faster, or even in different directions, than others?'*) to a form that, rather than asking them the question *'Do you think …'*, actually *causes* them to think.

This may be achieved by using a statement rather than a question, and one that has a more reflective nature, as in: *'I'm wondering about the way the clouds move. Some of them seem to go faster than others, or even in different directions …'* Such a discontinued self-statement has the inevitable effect of causing the listener to similarly ponder the dynamics of apparent cloud movement.

However, the real beauty of this format is that it actively avoids the unhelpful and undesired response of *'I don't know'* — one of the legitimate answers to any 'what', 'why', 'how', 'who' or 'when' questions, and one that specifically closes the thinking down.

The thinking process

When children ask questions, are we really obliged to provide them with answers? Is this a legitimate teaching role and does it achieve a useful outcome? Perhaps not.

When our children *ask* questions, it is therefore suggested that we *refrain from answering,* that we refrain from stealing their natural inclination to process, and that we verbally respond by actively *reflecting* on their question and the observations behind it.

We can liken the thinking process to the digging of a hole. When is a hole deep enough? The hole always has a bottom, but what could be beyond this? What happens if we dig one spadeful deeper? Is what we now see and understand (know) the full and final point, or is there a greater and perhaps quite different understanding just one spadeful of thinking deeper?

The human brain enjoys sense and fit, and it does not rest happily with things that do not make sense and that do not fit. This is why we sometimes find ourselves puzzling for extended periods of time over irrelevancies in our day-to-day life, on and on until we finally make sense of them, perhaps even years later. (As a teaching strategy it is sometimes useful to deliberately leave students with notions that do not quite make sense, as a means to promote such brain-grinding mental-processing activity.)

At the same time, however, this human brain of ours can be seen to be rather lazy — or maybe it is a matter of it being 'tidy'. It likes to tie up loose ends and to have open ends closed. And if they can be readily closed, our brain will tend to take this easy option. Hence answers to questions are very appealing, especially if they are a close enough fit. (All boxes ticked, no need to work on it any more.) This is the very reason we often hold such convincing misunderstandings, and why we so vigorously defend our 'beliefs'.

In this there is a tendency for the human brain to pursue a question until it finds a plausible explanation and then to move on, accepting that explanation at face value. In this way, 'answers' and 'goals' can serve to truncate our thinking process.

This is the reason we accumulate so many semi-understandings in life that serve to act as a ceiling, a cut-off point to our thinking, and which effectively prevent the further thinking that would lead to more full and more useful knowledge — surely the ideal learning process.

General teacher guidelines: a quick summary

What sensitivities, strategies and skills might we see characterizing a class teacher who demonstrates a 'dyslexia-sensitive' personal and teaching style?

That teacher may be seen to do the following.

- Have the tolerance that is gained from insight.

- Give the child time to listen and to understand.
- Use clear pictorial language.
- Avoid language that gives confusing mental images.
- Avoid using or accepting labels such as ADD, ADHD, APD, CPD and the like.
- Avoid telling the child or their parents that the child is dyslexic.
- Describe the 'diesel' attributes instead.
- Help the child and parents understand the child's own processing style.
- Give the child a range of structures and processes to ease their difficulties.
- Be aware and tolerant of their lack of 'self-talk' and its implications.
- Remember the complexity of the pictorial thinking mode.
- Recognize difficulties in their own style and moderate them.
- Own their own assumptions and 'truths' regarding the teaching/learning process.
- Remember that dyslexia is a teaching difficulty — not a learning difficulty.

In our next chapter, we stay in the classroom and peel the covers off dyscalculia, dyspraxia and dysgraphia.

> **We fail as educators when we allow the language of instruction to disqualify the student.**

Chapter Eleven

Other members of the 'dys' community

This final chapter presents some comments on the presentation, origins and significance of the other associated members of the 'dys' community.

- Dyscalculia
- Dyspraxia and dysgraphia

Dyscalculia

In essence, dyscalculia is the name given to the difficulty children have with recognizing numerals and in working with number concepts. Although these children are not usually seen as being dyslexic as such, in this writer's view the dynamics and the origins are the same, with some dyslexic children having marked skill in basic maths, while others will be at the other end of the scale, perhaps being labelled dyscalculic.

To understand and dismantle the child's difficulty, we first need to get a breakdown understanding of what the child is attempting to learn. What we refer to simply as 'number skills' is really a complex mixture of visual/perceptual, practical and verbal skills.

Initially we must recognize that there is a difference between what we call 'numbers' and 'numerals'. We generally use the word 'number' incorrectly, where we should be using the word 'numeral'.

A 'number' is a specified or unspecified number of items. A 'numeral' is the written, printed or typed digit representing the number of items. In the statement 'There are two people', the printed word *two* indicates that the number of people can be represented by the numeral 2 — or the spoken word two. If we are presented with a number of items, we can determine how many there are by item-counting. The numeral written down then represents this identified, verified number of items.

Common usage has led us to blend these two concepts (words), and although this does not present a problem to most people, it does to the person who displays the 'diesel' style known as dyscalculia.

The initial difficulty for the 'diesel thinker' is that the numeral on the page does not in any direct way indicate the number it represents — it is simply a code (as are the letters of the alphabet) that we use. Whereas the Roman numerals can be seen to go some way to demonstrating the actual number of items (I, II, III), the Arabic system does not. It uses an agreed shape, a squiggle, that is accepted as representing a number, but there is nothing in terms of its shape or its form that would tell the reader what number it represents.

As a numeric code it has obvious benefits when recording number information, particularly when the number itself is large, but it can be problematic to persons not previously familiar with this numeric system.

Shape

When the Phoenicians developed the encryption system that we currently use to record words and numerals (now known as the Arabic system) they did so with insight and foresight. Most of the letters of the alphabet still reflect their original template — a shape-base that could be described as a figure of eight lying on its side for letters, and the figure of eight standing on end for numerals.

This template of origin can be most readily understood by visiting your local petrol station and examining the large price-display sign on the forecourt. There, displayed in electronic digit form, are the numerals — all based on the squared-off version of the figure of eight. We are all too familiar with this one.

Having determined that the numerals take their form from the basic figure-of-eight shape, we now need to look at *how* this shape is formed, what hand movements are typically used to create this shape, as this can have significant implications for some people. Here another set of dynamics comes into play, that of the hereditary left- or right-handedness of the individual concerned. Although some authorities still question this notion, long observation has convinced this author of the significance of a family history involving some left-handedness as a major causal factor in terms of the presentation of 'diesel/dyslexic' or dyscalculic difficulties.

While a right-handed person naturally prescribes the figure 8 starting at the top with an anticlockwise movement, and finishing from the bottom with a clockwise lower loop then connecting to the top, the left-hander has a natural style that follows the opposite direction. (Note that many left-handers will have learned to use the 'right-handed' technique in their primary schooling.) The 'left-handed' form will often be used by apparent right-handers who carry some degree of left-sidedness in their gene-pool — a legacy from a left-hander, perhaps some way back in the family tree — or who more recently has been forced to become 'right-handed'.

Apparent or not, this difference in natural style will sometimes cause significant confusion at a visual/perceptual level to the point where the child is unable to readily learn and retain the significance of the various numeral shapes.

For these children, repeated attempts at rote learning are unlikely to work, and their repeated failure will predictably lead to frustration, anger and eventually to depression. It is therefore very important that the child's teacher understands the complexity of the learning task and has some insights into the reasons why the child might find the task difficult.

Method

The following approach is presented as a guide only, but it is designed to sequentially take the child through the steps required to acquire a full understanding of our number/numeral system.

- We start by first assisting the child to count by rote to ten as an oral exercise. In this, what the child is reciting is the names of the numerals. 'One, two, three...'
- Having achieved comfort in this, we then teach them to apply this oral information to visual groups of items displayed in reality, e.g. a group of three chocolates, five apples, seven marbles, and so on. In this, the child is now applying the oral information on a perceptual basis, and verbally expressing the name of the numeral that represents the number of items they see before them.
- Having achieved this, our next step is to rearrange these same items into visual patterns: three items presented as a row (or a triangle), four items presented as a square, five as a square with a central point, and so on. This pattern

recognition allows the child to readily identify numbers of items (up to ten) without having to actually count the items, thus introducing the notion of layout shape indicating the actual number.

In order to reinforce the 'representational' element of the numeral system, our next move is to repeat the previous steps *using pictures of items*, as opposed to using real (e.g. an apple) items. This is a relatively small learning step and should be quite readily achieved, then repeated in a third form, using just *dots to represent* the items.

All the while the child is orally telling the number.

The next step is to record in print the word representing the number — one, two, three... and helping them associate the *written word* with the spoken word, both of which represent the original visual pattern of items; that is, a number of items. (Note: this exercise may be made easier for the child by printing the words in CAPITAL letters.)

Finally, when all of this is happily mastered (and this may take a matter of some days), we then add in the hardest piece: the *numeral* that represents the word that represents the item count of objects. (Yes, if you are a language person this will seem to be all back to front, or at least in the wrong sequence.)

Prior to doing this the child should be asked to copy a figure-of-eight pattern, and note should be taken of the direction in which the child prescribes the pattern — is it a left-handed direction, or a right-handed direction? (See following diagram for details.) Ideally the directionality used here should match the dominant-sidedness of the child; for a right-handed, right-eyed and right-footed child the right-sided style should be reinforced. If the child shows predominant left-sidedness, the left-sided style should be reinforced.

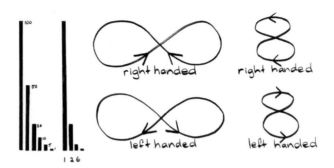

In assisting the child to finally master the figure of eight, and the individual numerals based on this shape, the Ron Davis (2010) technique of forming each of these numerals out of modelling clay or Plasticine may greatly facilitate the child's final mastery of the skill.

Using rods

This is really what our number system is all about, and truly it is quite remarkable that all of this is mastered very quickly by most children, and that only a few show difficulties at all.

However, there is yet another individual style factor that may need to be considered.

There is clear evidence that some people process number as a language concept while others see it as a visuo-spatial notion — they see specific number groups as blocks, or even as rods. Some people, especially savants, even add colour!

Some of us (whose age may be presented in greyish tones) were schooled in the use of coloured rods to represent specific number groups. The tallest rod might have been red and represented 100. A rod half of this height might have been green and represented 50. The next down represented 20, the next 10, the next 5, then 2, then 1.

This author — being specifically dyslexic and over 70 — still does all his mental arithmetic by visually shuffling an assortment of these rods in his pictorial mind, in a very fast and accurate manner.

It might be worth going to the trouble of locating or making a set of these (fine, square, wooden rods) so that your dyscalculic child is able to then start to process number (add, subtract, multiply) in a tactile (hands-on), visual (relative size, colour), spatial (relative position), verbal (the names), written (the numerals) manner.

This description of dyscalculia may not fit every child and this remedial approach may not work with every student. It pays to consider that every child is different, will have different needs, and will respond differently to any one approach.

Numerals to ten

Our mathematical system is based on groups of ten and units as part of a group of ten. The student who can see that addition, subtraction, multiplication and division are all based on units within groups of ten will find handling number (maths) relatively straightforward.

Dyslexic children typically learn best if they can 'see' and touch the material they are learning. In this they are visual and tactile processers, and so when assisting them in areas of difficulty it is wise to take this style into account. (Old-fashioned playing cards do just that!) It is interesting to note that many of the strategies and techniques that have been developed to assist these children have actually been developed from observation of what adult 'dyslexics' do in similar situations.

By way of example Paul (aged 42) explains his technique of turning numerals into pictures.

'I picture each numeral and the number it represents as a proportion of ten. In my mind "1" looks like a single solid box, with nine shadowy boxes the same size stacked above it, forming a column. And "3" looks like a stack of three solid boxes, with seven shadowy boxes stacked above. When I see the numeral 3, this is the picture I see in my head.

'I see all the numerals up to ten as this sort of pile. I see 100 and its ten divisions in the same way — and this makes adding, subtraction and multiplication really easy; I "see" what each number looks like, and what they look like in relation to each other.

'73 is two stacks side by side. The first stack has got seven solids with three shadowy ones above, and the second has got three solids and seven shadowy stacked above. Maths was very confusing until I taught myself to see each number as its part of a pile of ten.'

In order to help a child learn to 'see' numbers and numerals this way, start off by helping them recognize the 'caveman's calculator' — the fingers of both hands.

One lot of all the fingers of both hands, but with no extras, is recorded by the numerals 1 and 0, and appears as 10. One lot of ten and no more.

One lot of all the fingers of both hands, and two extras, is recorded as 1 and 2, and appears as 12.

Two lots of all the fingers of both hands, plus four extras, is recorded as 2 and 4, and appears as 24.

Maths and oral/printed language

Can mathematical or number concepts really be adequately presented via oral or printed language?

Most preschool children learn their basic number skills at a tactile and practical level. They learn what one finger is, and they learn what two fingers look like. They learn to rote count to ten, and gradually then learn to item count to ten, and eventually they learn to record the appropriate numerals on paper. Each new level of learning is built on the previous stage. Up to a certain stage in a child's schooling history maths is presented as numerals written on paper, and for the language thinkers this makes a certain amount of sense and is readily mastered. Dyslexic children also usually master this, using techniques of their own devising.

However, at a certain point another level of complication is introduced, and for many this is where it all falls apart. When the school system introduces maths problems as a *linguistic exercise* — either oral or written — the children who think in pictures have a real disadvantage.

An actual example taken from a classroom setting will help clarify the point. The teacher presents a maths problem, either written or oral:

John takes two apples from the apple barrel.
Paul takes seven apples from the apple barrel.
Half the apples are still left in the barrel.
How many apples are left in the barrel?

On the surface this seems to be a reasonable exercise — and for 85 per cent of the children in a school it will be. But let's look at what happens with two specific students.

The language-operator student sees the word 'two' and changes it into 2. They do the same with 'seven' and add the two to get 9. They are told that this number amounts to half the original number, and they know that halves are equal, so they conclude that the answer must be 9, expressed as 'nine'.

The 'diesel/dyslexic' picture-thinking student listens to the sentence and in their mind's eye sees a boy and a barrel. The barrel may be blue, plastic. They see a boy (John) approach the barrel and take an apple in each hand — and probably starts to eat one.

Another boy (Paul) then enters the scene and starts to grab apples from the barrel. He gets several out, but keeps trying to get more, drops some and apples are starting to roll around the floor. The first boy keeps munching his apple while the second is scrambling around the floor chasing apples. (It is important for us to recognize that this is because there is no visual concept of seven.)

The child is told that half the apples are still left in the barrel, but their pictorial brain can get no picture for this. There is no visual concept for the words 'half the apples', so their mind substitutes the closest pictorial approximation, which is a picture of 'half an apple' — neatly cut with the core displayed.

In their mind's eye John is still munching, Paul is still chasing rogue apples across the floor, and our student is faced with the visual image of half an apple. In response to the final question, they look in the barrel to see that, as stated, there is half an apple in there. Sure enough, there it is, neatly cut with the core showing.

So their answer is 'half', or at best 'half an apple'.

Nobody knows what has gone on in their processing. Nobody knows how the language has created chaos in their brain, and nobody could guess why they answered 'half', let alone what they meant by that. The teacher is likely to conclude that the child didn't try to work out the answer and just put down a silly response. She is not impressed and has no idea of how to work usefully with this child.

It is my observation that in real-life situations the practical application of mathematics is seldom a problem for 'diesel/dyslexic' people. Their difficulty lies in the classroom setting where practical maths has been hijacked and converted into a confusing language exercise. In using such clumsy mechanisms to teach children 'number skills', it may be that our main achievement is rather to effectively teach them that they are 'dumb and stupid'.

There are many well-established methods of helping children master number concepts (e.g. card games and the like), and teachers are encouraged to have a range (of non-computer-based strategies) available within the classroom. The scope of this particular chapter is not to teach the teacher how to teach, but simply to highlight and clarify why it is that the child may be experiencing difficulty in the first place.

Dyspraxia and dysgraphia

Along with the label dyslexic, it is now more and more common to find our children labelled as being dyspraxic and dysgraphic.

While it was once sufficient to regard a child as having difficulty with maths and number skills, or as being 'clumsy' or even 'poorly coordinated', and as having poor writing skills (terms which are readily understood), diagnostic and therapeutic interventions now deem them to be dyscalculic, dyspraxic and dysgraphic. With their Latin base, such labels give a pseudo-medical slant to the situation, insinuate some specific deficiency, and clearly depict the child as being deviant from the norm. Impressive, but not particularly kind or useful. To be clumsy or poor at maths was socially acceptable, but to be seen as dyspraxic or dysgraphic is to medicalize the topic, and to invite the thin edge of social prejudice — as well as a potential array of therapeutic intrusion to 'fix' the child.

Some parents and teachers argue that without these labels, assistance with funding and resources for these children would be minimal. This belief presumes that the labels do specify and clarify the issue sufficiently so as to actually help in accessing both funding and useful resources. Others more cynically note from sad experience that the presence of the labels achieves little in extra resources and ironically causes teachers and prospective employers (the label doesn't just wash off when the child turns sixteen!) to unconsciously dismiss the child as somehow being in deficit, and as having specialist needs — and therefore being of 'also-ran' status. It always pays to remember that the parent might choose the label but the child has to wear it.

Moving beyond the notion that many of these labels focus only on one end of a continuum of ability (the 'problematic' end), and that they are typically used and applied by people who have never personally experienced the difficulties themselves, we would note here that in this writer's experience there is a common source to this group of thinking and learning styles. They can all be seen to be different permutations of a basic dyslexia, having their origins in a natural personal inclination to favour pictorial rather than linguistic thinking.

Dyspraxia: where does it fit in?

Dyspraxia is another one of those confusing labels. A Google search yields the following definition: 'Dyspraxia (apraxia) — poor coordination displayed by some children. Diagnosed by illegible handwriting and inability to catch a ball — and clap the hands while the ball is in the air. Sometimes accompanies dyslexia.'

Discussion with a 'coordination therapist' suggests a much wider definition which involves:

- poor body/space awareness
- poor hand/fine-motor control
- difficulties with articulation (speech impediments) associated with the muscles of the tongue
- poor hand–eye coordination, and
- a lack of 'lateral' coordination — which includes
  - diminished left/right coordination,
  - poor front/back (of body) coordination, and
  - poor top/bottom (of body) coordination.

But what is it, and what might a parent or teacher see in a child that would point to the child being dyspraxic?

A lifetime of working with such children as an educational psychologist has revealed the following:

- Their speech is often indistinct, or they show an overt speech impediment.
- They commonly walk with shoulders down and hands hanging loose — not swinging as in a march, a skill they may never master.
- They walk 'from the hips down' — not involving their upper body.
- They frequently have great difficulty working out *left* from *right*.
- Their handwriting and printing can be very messy, untidy or spidery and can change from day to day.
- However, on the other hand, when we help them engage a different part of their brain, they may well be able to draw, or turn handwriting into an art form (calligraphy).
- Their printing often involves a mixture of capitals and lower-case letters, and they often prefer to type in capitals — and THEY ARE NOT YELLING AT YOU!

- They frequently are clumsy, bump into people or things, and are unintentionally heavy-handed or 'butter-fingered'. Breakages are common.
- They may be non-sporty, or get involved in 'full-body' sports (e.g. rugby league) — but do not do so well in hand–eye sports (e.g. tennis).

Some children do respond well to activities that are introduced sequentially and in a supportive manner (such as kapa haka), where expressive and rhythmical action is accompanied by music, or even rap. Physio and occupational therapy are generally well resourced in this regard.

A cautionary note. The real test of any intervention or support programme is the simple question to the child: '*Is this working for you?*' If the child answers in the negative, we may simply be extending their experience of failure, persecuting them for their difficulties, and be in danger of creating resistance, resentment, anger and depression. Remember, 'help' indicates failure.

Dysgraphia

A Google search generates a predictably varied set of definitions for dysgraphia, but fortunately they do overlap sufficiently to indicate that this label is used to describe people who seem to be unable to learn to write (print) well. We used to call it 'messy' handwriting and it was not a big deal as typewriters and laptops gave us a simple solution. Despite the problem-solving impact of advancing technology in this regard, its problematic potential is now kept alive through the use of such grandiose labelling.

Most definitions refer to an 'impaired ability' to form the shapes of the letters on paper, and some relate this to neuromuscular difficulties, others to 'brain dysfunction', and yet others to neither.

As the reader will by now predict, our view here is that such difficulties originate in motor-coordination confusion based in a mixture of left- and right-handedness, and readers are referred to the explanations given above on dyscalculia, involving the origins and use of the figure-of-eight shape by the Phoenicians in developing our alphabetic and numeric systems.

Over and above this, I see no reason why even the youngest children should not learn keyboard skills and be encouraged to use these skills right through their schooling lives, and beyond. Surprisingly, very few of us as adults ever seem to have any real need in our day-to-day life for 'neat' handwriting. This requirement, like the extraordinary historical focus on accurate spelling, although perhaps important in the past, may now need to be reconsidered.

> **Education is the only business where,**
> **if the customer does not buy the product,**
> **we fire the customer.**
> **— Anonymous**

The last word

Far from being the 'reading and writing' issue that dyslexia is often dismissed as this common information-processing style, 'dyslexia', is different from the norm and, for the individual, exists as a *daily life issue*. It impacts every aspect of life, creating stresses and difficulties that can erode a person's self-concept, and cripple their social interaction and consequent life satisfaction.

Similarly, if we regard dyslexia as a 'learning difficulty', we are guilty of blaming the victim, of denying the huge, hidden bulk of the dyslexia iceberg, and of cheating the student, their family and the teachers of a full and rewarding life.

The 'diesel' pictorial thinking style is present in varying degrees in approximately 15 per cent of our population — up to five children in every classroom in our schools. It is a common, valid and valued processing style, and only becomes problematic because of the unrecognized educational emphasis on language as the main vehicle of learning in our current educational system.

This emphasis on language as the basic tool of learning for *all* children in their early years is a relatively recent development and, ironically, is being progressively advanced as educators struggle to identify and resolve the deficits in the system. Their efforts to solve the problem are actually compounding the situation.

With their hidden implicit belief that language is the preferred, if not the singular, vehicle for processing information in our junior schools, our educators are unwittingly guilty of robbing our predominantly pictorial thinkers of success in the classroom — and thereby of qualifications and legitimacy in life.

We must consult with, and listen to, the ones who have been disadvantaged through our lack of understanding.

The last, last word

Client feedback: what the students want from us

The over-riding message of this book is that, even with the best intentions, we can misinterpret and therefore misjudge the diesel/dyslexic child. The intention is that, with useful insight and information, we can develop a more sensitive, a more supportive, and a more useful understanding of the child. However, even with this information, it is both predictable and acceptable that the classroom teacher will ask, 'What can I do to help circumvent all of this? Is there anything that will assist the child to move past these difficulties?'

Although it is now seen to be more acceptable to consult with students about educational issues, it is very evident that the students who are consulted with are the ones who are articulate, confident, and 'user-friendly' to the system. Perhaps we should consider throwing our net a little wider.

The constant feedback from the children themselves indicates that the most significant useful impact comes from the personal style of the teacher, and the teacher and parent refraining from inadvertently making the child's school life miserable — the implicit message being that the 'help' that is so often given to the dyslexic child is sheer torture in itself.

So, remaining true to our politically incorrect style, we leave the last words to the students themselves. Their messages include:

1. Please refrain from deliberate or inadvertent put-downs.
2. Recognise that we need more time to read, to listen and to think, and slower language of instruction.
3. Please don't be intolerant of us, and please accept that our difficulties are real.
4. We know you are frustrated by us, but please use a personal style (verbal and physical responses) that conveys a positive attitude and acceptance:
   - Address us by name.
   - Smile when you interact with us.
   - Ask us to give you more information when you are confused by what we say.
   - Make sure you use of the word 'yes' more often than you use the word 'no'.
   - Totally avoid the use of the words 'Wrong', 'Don't', 'Just' and 'Try'.
   - When we are having difficulty with something, please don't tell us that 'It is easy, you just…'. This really hurts.
   - We like to be liked, too — let us know that you actually like us. It's okay to use affectionate terms such as 'honey', 'love', 'buddy', 'mate'.
   - We know you have to be careful, but most of us also like to be touched.
5. At the end of the day check in with us about how it was for us.
6. Give us a bigger range of ways to express ourselves, and to indicate our opinion and our knowledge:
   - acting out scenarios
   - small group discussions

- the use of drawings, magazine pictures, illustrations, YouTube clips, actual demonstration
- mind maps as a working tool
- bullet points instead of full writing
- journalism techniques (writing down, then writing up)
- lessons and techniques in essay writing.

7. We are creative and imaginative, and enjoy the use of freeform acting (involving clown's noses, masks, hats, dress-ups, etc.). When we are shy, this may allow us to find safe ways to practise social interaction and act in different ways.

8. We are often waiting for you to encourage us to participate in school drama productions, local theatre, acting groups, drama groups. We don't have the confidence to do it alone.

9. Support us to join dance, music, martial arts, Scouts, Air Cadets, nature groups, conservation groups, etc. Most of us want to be involved, but don't know how.

Thank you for listening.

Appendix: Interventions

A further offering on aspects of the world of the 'diesel/dyslexic' person.

Yes, we know we have these children in our homes and in our classrooms.

Yes, we now have a reasonable idea what they look like and can even think of specific children who may well be 'diesels' — and even some in our own classroom.

Yes, we also have a reasonable idea of what it is that makes them the way they are — the way their brains are wired, the way they think.

Yes, we accept that with the right approaches they can be achievers in our system.

But how do we work with them? How do we intervene in a useful way without making them feel 'special' or negatively different?

The range of possible interventions can be seen to be based on several dynamics including:

- The student: their current beliefs about themselves; their style of learning, processing, thinking; their current manifesting difficulties.
- The teacher: their personal style, their beliefs about the student; their use and understanding of teaching technique.

- The identified problem area, which could include any,
  or all, of:
  - Reading, writing, comprehension, verbal interaction,
    social, employment-based, domestic, behaviour,
    emotional, relationship — or what we otherwise call *life*;
    and
  - The professional and philosophical constraints of the
    particular educational establishment.

Our discussion here, though, will be largely constrained to a focus
on the student concerned.

It is a given fact that, by the time a student has been identified
as needing assistance, they will have endured a personal history of
experiences that will have led them to have certain beliefs about
themselves — of which they may or may not be aware, depending
perhaps, on their age.

Such school-age children most commonly see themselves as
being 'dumb', 'naughty', 'lazy', 'bad' and a host of other descriptors,
depending on how much parents and teachers have used the
cajoling and blaming approach as an initial means to rectify the
'problem'.

Unfortunately, simply telling a child that they are *not* these
things ('You are not dumb, not lazy, not bad, not naughty') is
unlikely to have any useful effect at all, because by this time the
child will have associated these labels (dumb, lazy, bad, naughty)
with their own observed performance, and predictably will have
seen and accepted the correlation as being valid.

Similarly, the child will just hear empty words when you assure
them that they are smart, clever, talented, lovable — and the other
'prop-up' attempts we make. Yes, the child may be a talented artist,
a brilliant rugby player, fleet of foot or whatever, but if they are

struggling with the linguistic educational basics such as reading and writing, hearing and understanding, your words are unlikely to ever enter the barricaded doors that protect their emotional realm.

We need to understand that these children will need evidence that is *valid in their own eyes* before they will start to relinquish such old beliefs, and even begin to consider that they are personally okay, and that there may be a different reason for their frustrations and difficulties. What we the adults do and how we do it becomes highly significant at this point.

In order to allow the child to move on, and up, we must release them from the constraints of a collapsed self-concept. We must understand that it is the child's belief systems, particularly their beliefs about themselves (their self-concept), that are most significant now in limiting or determining their performance ability.

However, changing the child's performance evidence will not in itself change their beliefs — erratic success is a very dangerous thing for the child who believes they are different. If their self-concept tells them that they are dumb or stupid, they will moderate their performance to match this and revert to a 'failure' style in order to achieve an inner balance, an ironic position of safety.

To avoid this, and to achieve a different outcome, the child therefore needs to be able to consider a *different story*. Our initial task as parent, teacher or counsellor is to create a space that will allow for a change in the mindset of the child, and this can be initiated by feeding in information that they are unlikely or unable to refute. One way to do this is by telling stories. So, we recommend the use of stories.

Stories don't have to be true, nor do they need to be personally challenging. They can just subtly illustrate a point, and in doing so indicate the possibility of a different perception, a different way of looking at things. This technique has been modelled repeatedly and successfully by the great religious teachers down through time. The stories told by Jesus, by Buddha, by Aesop and others are well known today, despite their antiquity.

Most children immediately grasp the implications of the idea that some of us are 'petrols' and that some of us are 'diesels'. This then paves the way for an examination of different thinking styles (linguistic/pictorial) via the use of two laptop computers — one showing linguistic information and the other pictorial information.

This in itself can be shown to equate to the two sides of the brain and their generalized functioning, all of which then allows the child to eventually conclude: '*I am a diesel, and they are trying to feed me petrol. No wonder I find it confusing and hard. No wonder it does not make sense.*'

Now the child has a different frame via which to see themselves and can start to assess themselves differently. Slowly they can abandon their old self-concept and start to re-evaluate the evidence about their own life in a more positive and useful way.

Fortunately, this works with children, and it is equally useful with adults, who will often be able to change their mindset in the time it has taken the reader to read this page.

In countries where the average person has less acquaintance with internal-combustion engines and their different fuelling systems, a little more groundwork may need to be done first to familiarize the person with 'petrol/diesel' implications.

If the student's current difficulties are academic, those implications need to be examined. If the difficulties are social-behavioural (maybe counselling directed by a court of law), or relate to marital relationships, then how the 'diesel/petrol' dynamic applies to these contexts needs to be examined.

Here the *dual brain continuum* comes into its own as a pictorial tool to demonstrate how, and at what point, the student's difficulties occur. It is certainly helpful if the parents of the child understand this diagrammatic tool, and it is interesting to see how instrumental the child often is in helping the parents achieve a useful understanding of the model.

References and further reading

Burridge, Kate, *Blooming English: Observations on the roots, cultivation and hybrids of the English language*, ABC Books, Sydney, 2002.

Davis, Ron, *The Gift of Dyslexia: Why some of the smartest people can't read ... and how they can learn*, third edition, Pedigree/ Penguin, New York, 2010.

Gray, John, *Men are from Mars, Women are from Venus: The classic guide to understanding the opposite sex*, HarperCollins, New York, 1992.

Hoopmann, Kathy, *All Dogs have ADHD*, Jessica Kingsley Publishers, London, 2008.

King, Laughton, *Reaching the Reluctant Learner*, third edition, Self-Published, New Zealand, 2006.

King, Laughton, *With, Not Against*, second edition, Self-Published, New Zealand, 2008.

King, Laughton, *Dyslexia Dismantled*, Self-Published, New Zealand, 2010.

Pease, Allan and Barbara, *Why Men Don't Listen and Women Can't Read Maps: How we are different and what to do about it*, Broadway Books, New York, 2001.

Tolle, Eckhart, *A New Earth: Awakening to your life's purpose*, Penguin, New York, 2005.

Index